**THE NATIONAL PARKS**

Poster created under the Works Progress Administration in 1940 to boost tourism to the national parks

**YELLOWSTONE NATIONAL
PARK | WYOMING**
......................................

Great Fountain Geyser both
eclipses and reflects a pastel
sunset in the Lower Geyser
Basin in Wyoming's Yellowstone National Park, the
world's first—and to this day,
most famous—national park,
established in 1872.

# The NATIONAL
# PARKS

## *An Illustrated History*

## KIM HEACOX

NATIONAL GEOGRAPHIC

WASHINGTON, D.C.

SEQUOIA NATIONAL
PARK | CALIFORNIA

A giant sequoia is a world
unto itself. This particular tree,
the President, at 3,200 years
old, was a seedling when
Moses led the Israelites from
Egypt to Canaan. It stands
247 feet high and has 534
limbs, with the largest branch
nearly 60 feet long. After
reaching its current height
more than 1,000 years ago,
it has grown in volume of
wood and developed a more
complex crown.

**GATES OF THE ARCTIC
NATIONAL PARK | ALASKA**

The Koyukuk River flows
off the south side of the
Brooks Range in Alaska's
eight-million-acre Gates of
the Arctic National Park,
where autumn arrives in
August. This entire park sits
north of the Arctic Circle.

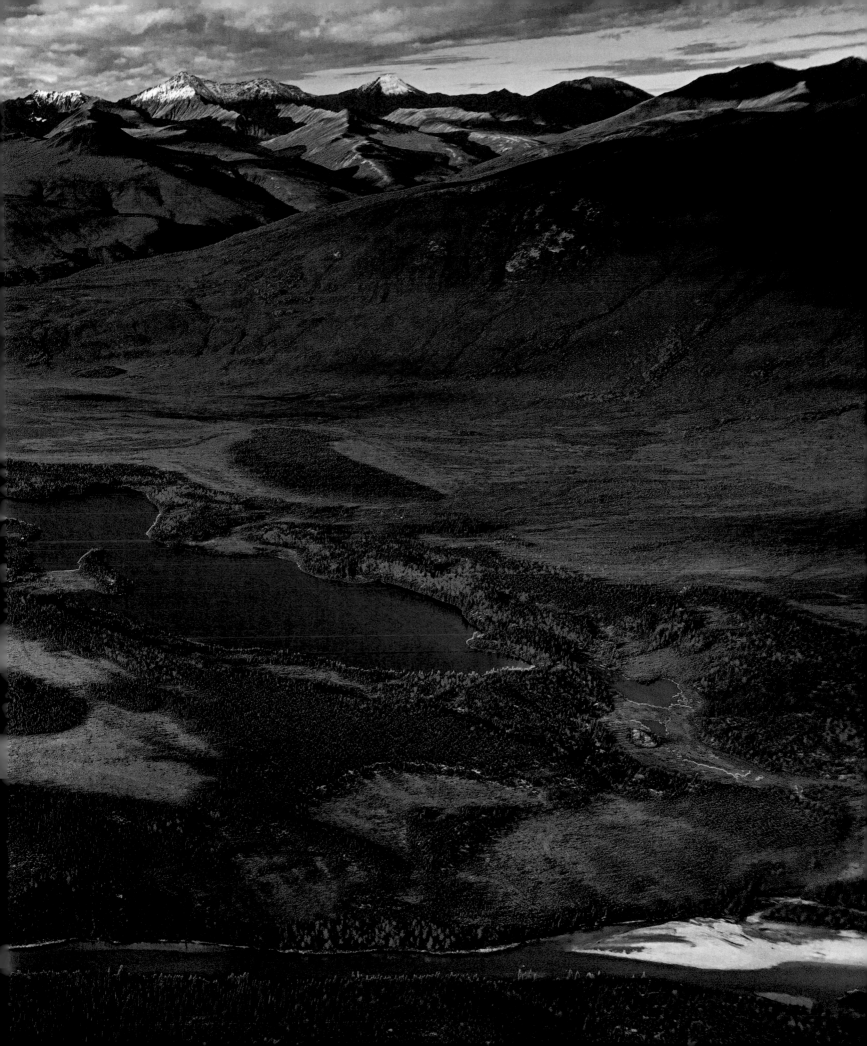

**LINCOLN MEMORIAL**
**WASHINGTON, D.C.**

...............................................

"With malice toward none, with charity for all"—the words and deeds of Abraham Lincoln, 16th president of the United States and the "savior" of the nation, remain vivid today, enshrined in the Lincoln Memorial, in the heart of Washington, D.C.

# Panel of Experts

---

## *National Parks Consultants*

NATIONAL GEOGRAPHIC IS PROUD TO have worked collaboratively with the National Park Service to develop this book. The National Parks Centennial Committee—including Alexa Viets, Donald Leadbetter, Monique Vanlandingham, Lynne Murdock, and Duey Kol—shared advice and excellent information, for which we're grateful. In addition, four individuals contributed vast amounts of institutional knowledge and expertise and were involved in the creation of this book from the very beginning to the very end. Their combined service to, and association with, the national parks totals more than 100 years, and we are indebted to their contribution. In alphabetical order, they are:

## DENIS P. GALVIN

After serving in the first Peace Corps group in Tanganyika, Denis P. Galvin joined the National Park Service at Sequoia National Park in 1963 as a civil engineer. In a 38-year career, he served in parks, regional offices, training centers, and service centers. He concluded his NPS career with 16 years in the Washington office, where he served as deputy director for 9 years. As the highest ranking career official, he represented the agency in over 200 congressional hearings. Since his 2002 retirement, he has remained active in the conservation field, serving on numerous commissions and as a lecturer and consultant. He is currently a trustee of the National Parks Conservation Association.

## T. DESTRY JARVIS

T. Destry Jarvis has spent the past 40 years working and consulting in national park units, recreation, cooperative land use, public lands natural and cultural resources, historic preservation, and youth service fields. Currently the president of Outdoor Recreation and Park Services, Jarvis has also served as the executive director of the National Recreation and Park Association; vice president of the National Association of Service and Conservation Corps; assistant director of the U.S. National Park Service; executive vice president of the Student Conservation Association; and vice president of the National Parks Conservation Association.

## JOHN H. SPRINKLE, JR.

After a decade of private sector experience in historic preservation and environmental policy, John H. Sprinkle, Jr., joined the National Park Service in late 1998 and currently serves as the agency's bureau historian. During his tenure, he helped direct both the National Historic Landmarks Program (where he shepherded nominations for Tennessee's Ryman Auditorium, Sun Studios, and Graceland) and the Federal Preservation Institute. Sprinkle holds a Ph.D. in American history from the College of William and Mary and is the author of *Crafting Preservation Criteria: The National Register of Historic Places and American Historic Preservation.*

## ROBERT K. SUTTON

Robert K. Sutton assumed the duties of chief historian of the National Park Service in October 2007 after serving as the Superintendent of Manassas National Battlefield Park for 12½ years. From 1986 to 1990, he directed the Historic Preservation and Historical Administration public history programs at Arizona State University. He has published a number of books, articles, and reviews on various public history topics. One of his primary interests at Manassas Battlefield and in his current position has been preparing for the sesquicentennial of the Civil War, and as part of that effort, he has encouraged Civil War battlefields to expand their interpretive programs to focus more attention to the social, economic, and political issues during the Civil War era.

# Contents

———◈———

**YOSEMITE NATIONAL PARK
CALIFORNIA**

......................................

Cathedral Rocks stands
perfectly reflected in the still
waters of Yosemite Valley,
in Yosemite National Park.
For generations, artists,
writers, scientists, teachers,
students, rangers, and rock
climbers have found challenge
and inspiration in the granite
spires, domes, and sheer vertical faces of this famous park.

# Foreword

---✦---

*Jonathan B. Jarvis,*
*Director, National Park Service*

IT BEGAN AS A PROPOSAL THAT I THOUGHT WAS FOOLISH: Five guys in wheelchairs wanted to climb Guadalupe Peak, the highest point in Texas and the iconic center of Guadalupe Mountains National Park. As the Frijole District ranger, I knew the hike well; it's a rugged grind of steep switchbacks and sheer drop-offs, gaining 3,000 feet over four miles in the heat of the desert. Plus, in my Chihuahua desert park, everything alive stings, bites, has thorns, or is poisonous. My recommendation was "no way," but they came anyway. Over the following five days, I watched five tough and determined men start the climb and three make the 9,000-foot summit, dragging themselves and their chairs up the mountain as an unaided team. And I witnessed, perhaps for the first time, how our national parks challenge us to achieve things we never thought possible, to overcome overwhelming odds, and to work together toward a common goal. This was early in my career, and it set in motion a belief that our parks are more than just pretty places. They have the power to change people and perhaps, in aggregate, guide our society in this great experiment in democracy. That concept has been my driver for the 40 years I have served the National Park Service as a ranger, biologist, superintendent, and regional director, and now as its 18th director.

Over those four decades, I have had more rich experiences than anyone deserves, each reinforcing this belief that the power of our national parks and the ideas they represent are essential to the fabric of our nation. In those extraordinary moments, I can be overwhelmed with the responsibility of our stewardship of these places, their stories, and their value to our country, if not the world.

In the early morning of December 7, 1941, sailors were gathering for breakfast when the first Japanese bombs exploded over the mess hall.

**FREDERICK DOUGLASS PEN AND INKWELL STAND**

**FREDERICK DOUGLASS NATIONAL HISTORIC SITE, WASHINGTON, D.C.**

..................................................

"If there is no struggle, there is no progress," wrote the African-American social reformer and statesman Frederick Douglass (1818-95), perhaps while using a pen and 14-inch-tall inkstand similar to this one, on display today at the Frederick Douglass National Historic Site.

The U.S.S. *Arizona* sank at her mooring with 1,102 men aboard. They are still there. Years later, we slipped into the murky water of Pearl Harbor, donned our masks and respirators, and descended on the imposing hulk. As we swam along the collapsed deck, plates, silverware, and pots and pans were strewn about. My dive partner, an NPS underwater archaeologist, motioned me over to an intact cook pot. With his finger, he wiped away the skim of algae to reveal the NPS collection number, indicating that every item accessible on this ship had been assessed, tagged, and entered into our inventory, recording it for research, interpretation, preservation, and respect for those who died on that day that, in the words of FDR, "will live in infamy." Each year as we gather on December 7, with our friends from Japan at our side, we pledge to the Pearl Harbor survivors, now dwindling to only a few, that we will never let America or the world forget.

The NPS faces significant challenges as it looks to its second century, but I am optimistic about our next 100 years, as the NPS has a history of extraordinary accomplishments despite daunting odds.

During my four decades, we returned the wolf to Yellowstone and restored its natural quiet, reintroduced natural fire to many western ecosystems, and created the first marine wilderness. We restored passive flow to the Everglades, took down dams blocking a river in Olympic National Park, and moved our own visitor development out of the giant sequoias. We pioneered landscape level conservation, recognizing our parks as anchors in connected ecosystems. We shifted our interpretation at Civil War sites to the role of slavery and the contemporary fight for civil rights, and we added many new parks that focus on the stories of our American experience that are difficult but essential to tell. We elevated women to the highest level of leadership of the Park Service and recognized that our urban national parks are the centers of innovation and the gateways to a new generation of diverse park visitors, supporters, and advocates. We grew our "friends" organizations into philanthropic partners, raising millions to support park programs. And we increased our role in informal public education, taking on the complex issue of climate change. We asserted that the climate is changing, that it is caused by human activities, and that our national parks are natural solutions. Oh, and by the way, in my 40 years at the Park Service, we cumulatively hosted approximately eight billion visits by the public, a number greater than the human population of the world in 2014. I could go on and on, but I use these only as reminders that we have risen to challenges before, and we succeed because we must—it is our mission. I could not be more proud of this great institution and my ability to have played some small role in our many achievements.

I know that our second century will be successful, because regardless of how ethnically diverse, distracted, urban, and technologically addicted this next generation may be, the NPS still has something to offer that they cannot get anywhere else. Recently, a young man was participating in a youth experience program at Grand Teton National Park. It was his first time there, and in many ways he represents the emerging U.S. population: urban, diverse, inexperienced in the national parks. He stopped his bicycle along the path, and while gazing at the Teton sunrise, broke into tears. If we could collect those tears (Harry Potter–like) and read their history and meaning, I know we would see a life changed, a self-discovery, and a positive promise for this young man because of his National Park experience. While the National Park Service did not create the Teton mountains, we did and will continue to fight for their protection as a National Park, so that every American now and in future generations can stand shoulder to shoulder equally with their fellow citizens and have that moment of emotional discovery about their country and themselves.

While seeing our national parks through books will never replace the real experience, this excellent new National Geographic book presents a vivid and complete picture of the NPS and its mission in a way that will inform and encourage the American people to visit and support their parks through our second century. ■

**MOUNT RUSHMORE NATIONAL MEMORIAL SOUTH DAKOTA**

...................................

At Mount Rushmore National Memorial, visitors admire the likeness of four U.S. presidents (left to right): George Washington, Thomas Jefferson, Theodore Roosevelt, and Abraham Lincoln. Sculpted into solid granite more than a mile above sea level (elevation 5,725 feet) by Danish-American Gutzon Borglum, the work began in 1927 and ended in 1941. Each presidential face is roughly 60 feet tall.

# BY THE NUMBERS

FROM AN ANNUAL VISITATION of only a few thousand in 1916 to nearly 300 million in 2016, the national parks have grown immensely in total acreage and popularity. They represent freedom, adventure, diversity, dedication, respect, and restraint. ■

## 292,800,082
2014 recreational visits

## 167,000,000
⌄ Objects in museum collections

Globe, Lincoln Home National Historic Site

## 84,000,000
Acres of land

## 660,000
"Junior Rangers"

## 246,000
Volunteers

## 75,000
Archaeological sites

## 27,000
Historic and prehistoric structures

## 20,000
Employees

## 18,000
Miles of trails

## 407
Total number of park properties

## 247
Endangered plants and animals

## 78
National monuments

## 59
National parks

## 25
Battlefields

## 10
Seashores

## 4
New parks added in 2014

## OLD SCHOOL

# ADMISSION (ZOO) STICKERS

DESIGNED FOR WINDSHIELDS, national park admission "zoo" stickers—showing animals—became popular in the 1920s and 1930s. As avid park visitors filled their windshields, the stickers created a safety hazard and were discontinued in 1940. ■

BEHIND THE SYMBOLS

# WHAT THE LOGO REPRESENTS

**ARROWHEAD FORM:** the nation's diverse peoples and the richness of our shared experience

**MOUNTAINS, TREES, AND LAKE:** the complexity and beauty of our natural landscape

**BISON:** the animals that share and enrich our environment and help to connect the NPS logo to the Department of the Interior's seal

THE INDIVIDUAL ELEMENTS of the National Park Service's arrowhead logo (described above) have come to symbolize the agency's efforts to protect our natural and cultural heritage. Over the years, other logos have come into use (below) that sought to modernize the Park Service and its mission, but none have had the staying power of the now iconic arrowhead. ■

2001

BEFORE 1952

1952

1966

2001

*Top row, left to right:* Acadia, Bryce Canyon, Cedar Breaks, Crater Lake, Death Valley, Devils Tower, General Grant, Glacier, Grand Canyon, Grand Teton; *bottom row, left to right:* Hot Springs, Lassen Volcanic, Mesa Verde, Mt. Rainier, Pinnacles, Platt, Rocky Mountain, Sequoia, Wind Cave, Yellowstone, Yosemite, Zion

# MOST VISITED PARKS

WHILE GREAT SMOKY MOUNTAINS WAS the most visited national park in 2014, the most visited of all NPS properties was the Golden Gate Recreation Area. Below are the rest of the top 10 parks (out of 59) and park properties (out of 407). ∎

| ALL PARK PROPERTIES | LOCATION | VISITORS |
|---|---|---|
| Golden Gate National Recreation Area | California | 15,004,420 |
| Blue Ridge Parkway | Virginia, North Carolina | 13,941,749 |
| Great Smoky Mountains National Park | North Carolina, Tennessee | 10,099,276 |
| George Washington Memorial Parkway | Washington, D.C., Maryland, Virginia | 7,472,150 |
| Lincoln Memorial | Washington, D.C. | 7,139,072 |
| Lake Mead National Recreation Area | Arizona, Nevada | 6,942,873 |
| Gateway National Recreation Area | New York, New Jersey | 6,021,713 |
| Natchez Trace Parkway | Alabama, Mississippi, Tennessee | 5,846,474 |
| Chesapeake and Ohio Canal National Historical Park | Washington, D.C., Maryland, West Virginia | 5,066,219 |
| Grand Canyon National Park | Arizona | 4,756,771 |
| NATIONAL PARKS | LOCATION | VISITORS |
| Great Smoky Mountains National Park | North Carolina, Tennessee | 10,099,276 |
| Grand Canyon National Park | Arizona | 4,756,771 |
| Yosemite National Park | California | 3,882,642 |
| Yellowstone National Park | Idaho, Montana, Wyoming | 3,513,484 |
| Rocky Mountain National Park | Colorado | 3,434,751 |
| Olympic National Park | Washington | 3,243,872 |
| Zion National Park | Utah | 3,189,696 |
| Grand Teton National Park | Wyoming | 2,791,392 |
| Acadia National Park | Maine | 2,563,129 |
| Glacier National Park | Montana | 2,338,528 |

**GOLDEN GATE NATIONAL RECREATION AREA | CALIFORNIA**
The Golden Gate Bridge, a centerpiece of Golden Gate National Recreation Area, joins San Francisco with Marin County.

## LIFE IN THE PARKS

# BIG ANIMALS

THE NATIONAL PARK SERVICE TAKES SERIOUSLY the preservation of healthy ecosystems and robust wildlife populations. From the massive American bison to the relatively petite mountain lion, below are a few of the larger, more charismatic species you may encounter in U.S. national parks and their maximum weights when fully grown. ■

**MUSK OX**
800 LBS

**WHITE-TAILED DEER**
300 LBS

**DALL SHEEP**
300 LBS

**MOOSE** 1,800 LBS

**BISON** 2,200 LBS

**BLACKTIP SHARK**
220 LBS

**AMERICAN ALLIGATOR**
1,000 LBS

**NURSE SHARK**
330 LBS

**CARIBOU**
700 LBS

**WOLF** 175 LBS

**BLACK BEAR**
600 LBS

**GRIZZLY BEAR**
800 LBS

**MOUNTAIN LION**
136 LBS

**ROOSEVELT ELK:** 1,100 LBS

**AMERICAN CROCODILE**
2,000 LBS

# AMERICAN SUPERLATIVES

NATIONAL PARKS AND OTHER PRESERVED SITES contain the biggest and the best of the American landscape, and the most profound elements of our past. Some sites don't require size to be profound; others are larger than their actual geography, and give us wings and room to soar. ■

Thaddeus Kosciuszko
National Memorial
0.02 acres

Brown vs. Board
of Education
National Historic Site
2 acres

Cane River Creole
National Historical Park
200 acres

Congaree
National Park
27,000 acres

Grand Teton
National Park
310,000 acres

## GOING TO EXTREMES

### THE LARGEST AND SMALLEST NATIONAL PARKS

Wrangell-St. Elias
National Park and Preserve
13,200,000 acres

Joshua Tree
National Park
800,000 acres

**HIGHEST POINT**

Denali (aka Mount McKinley), 20,320 feet in Alaska's Denali National Park

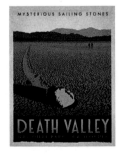

**LOWEST POINT**

Badwater Basin, 282 feet below sea level in California's Death Valley National Park

**DEEPEST LAKE**

Crater Lake, 1,943 feet deep in Oregon's Crater Lake National Park

**LONGEST CAVE**

Mammoth Cave, 400-plus miles in Mammoth Cave National Park

**TALLEST TREES**

Up to 379.7 feet high in California's Redwood National Park

**BEST WATERFALL**

Yosemite Falls, 2,425 feet high in California's Yosemite National Park

# A TIME LINE

THE HISTORY OF THE NATIONAL PARKS and the evolution of the U.S. National Park Service are inseparable. Each has grown, diversified, and matured in concert with the other and become a deep part of America's self-identity. Below are some highlights. ∎

**1864**: Lincoln signs the Yosemite Act, protecting the Mariposa Grove and Yosemite Valley—it is the first law ever passed in the United States to protect wild lands for the enjoyment of people.

**1868**: John Muir arrives in Yosemite for the first time.

**1869**: John Wesley Powell leads the first known expedition down the Colorado River through the Grand Canyon.

**MARCH 1, 1872**: President Ulysses S. Grant signs the Yellowstone Park Act into law, making Yellowstone America's first national park.

**OCTOBER 1, 1890**: Yosemite, Sequoia, and General Grant become national parks.

**1899**: Mount Rainier National Park is established as the first national park in the Pacific Northwest, and the first carved from a forest reserve.

**1906**: President Roosevelt signs the American Antiquities Act authorizing the establishment of national monuments by executive privilege—no congressional approval necessary.

**1910**: Glacier National Park is established, with its 125 glaciers. A century later, the park will have fewer than 25 glaciers.

**DECEMBER 1913**: President Woodrow Wilson signs legislation to dam the Tuolumne River and flood Hetch Hetchy Valley in Yosemite National Park.

**AUGUST 25, 1916**: The National Park Service is created with the passage of the "Organic Act," drafted by Frederick Law Olmsted, Jr.

**1917**: Stephen T. Mather becomes head of the National Park Service with Horace M. Albright as his assistant

**1920**: Annual visitation to the national parks exceeds one million.

**1926**: A citizen campaign among residents of Virginia, Tennessee, and North Carolina pays $2.5 million for Shenandoah National Park and $10 million for Great Smoky Mountains National Park.

**1929**: Wildlife biologist George Melendez Wright conceives of and personally funds the first comprehensive survey advocating for a scientific approach to wildlife management in the national parks.

**1930**: NPS hires its first professional historian, Vern Chatelain.

**1933**: A government reorganization transfers War Department battlefields, archaeological sites, historic sites, and parks in the nation's capital to the NPS. The expansion nearly doubles the number of units in the national park system.

**1935**: Congress directs the NPS to identify nationally significant historic sites for consideration as parks and creates the National Park System Advisory Board to advise the secretary of the interior on the designation of national historic sites.

**1941**: Ansel Adams begins photographing the national parks.

**1943**: George Washington Carver becomes the first national park to celebrate the accomplishments of an African American.

**1948**: Hampton National Historic Site is recognized solely for its architectural significance, a designation that leads to the establishment of the National Trust for Historic Preservation.

**1956**: A five-billion-dollar, ten-year program called Mission 66 begins. Its objective: to upgrade facilities, staffing, and resource management through the national park system.

**1960**: Ronald Lee develops the National Historic Landmark program to expand the recognition and protection of nationally significant historic properties.

**1966**: Congress establishes the National Register of Historic Places as the nation's official list of properties considered significant in our collective heritage.

**1968**: On an 800-acre site in Kings Canyon National Park, the Park Service ignites the first "prescribed burn."

**1972**: Yellowstone National Park celebrates its centennial; annual visitation to national parks exceeds 160 million.

**1972**: Congress creates Gateway (New York City) and Golden Gate (San Francisco), greatly expanding the urban presence of the NPS.

**1976**: Congress establishes the historic rehabilitation tax credit program. It has leveraged $69 billion in private investment toward the adaptive use of 40,000 historic properties.

**1980**: The birthplace of Martin Luther King, Jr., becomes a national historic site.

**1980**: Women's Rights National Historical Park is added to the system, commemorating women's struggle for equal rights.

**1988**: An epic fire burns one-third of Yellowstone (700,000 acres). The aftermath becomes a researcher's haven as three decades of rejuvenation begin to unfold.

**1992**: Manzanar, memorializing the detention of Japanese citizens during WWII, becomes a national historic site—the first to interpret difficult aspects of the nation's story,

**1995**: Wolves are reintroduced into Yellowstone after a 70-year absence. The health of many other park species begins to improve in ways that surprise visitors and scientists alike.

**2010**: The NPS develops a "Climate Change Response Strategy" for addressing and lessening the effects of climate change.

**2016**: The National Park Service turns 100, marking the moment with a massive celebration called Find Your Park. A century on, the system totals more than 400 NPS units, 59 of them national parks.

**WASHINGTON**

Olympic National Park
North Cascades National Park
Mount Rainier National Park
Glacier National Park

**OREGON**

Crater Lake National Park
Redwood National Park

**CALIFORNIA**

Lassen Volcanic National Park
Yosemite National Park
Pinnacles National Park
Kings Canyon N.P.
Sequoia N.P.
Death Valley National Park
Channel Islands National Park
Joshua Tree National Park

San Francisco

**NEVADA**

Great Basin National Park

**UTAH**

Capitol Reef National Park
Bryce Canyon N.P.
Zion National Park
Arches National Park
Canyonlands National Park

**ARIZONA**

Grand Canyon National Park
Petrified Forest National Park
Saguaro National Park

**MONTANA**

**IDAHO**

**WYOMING**

Yellowstone National Park
Grand Teton National Park

**COLORADO**

Rocky Mountain National Park
Black Canyon of the Gunnison National Park
Mesa Verde National Park
Great Sand Dunes National Park and Preserve

**NORTH DAKOTA**

Theodore Roosevelt National Park

**SOUTH DAKOTA**

Wind Cave National Park
Badlands National Park

**NEBRASKA**

**KANSAS**

**NEW MEXICO**

Carlsbad Caverns National Park
Guadalupe Mountains National Park

**TEXAS**

Big Bend National Park
Amistad Reservoir

**OKLA**

**MEXICO**

**CANADA**

PACIFIC OCEAN

Str. of Juan de Fuca
Columbia
Goose L.
Great Salt Lake
Utah L.
Lake Tahoe
Salton Sea
Colorado
Lake Mead
Lake Powell
Fort Peck Lake
Missouri
Lake Sakakawea
Lake Oahe
Lake Francis Case
Platte
Arkansas
Red
Pecos
Rio Grande

ROCKY MOUNTAINS
COAST RANGE
SIERRA NEVADA
GREAT BASIN
COLORADO PLATEAU

**ALASKAN PARKS**

ARCTIC OCEAN
BEAUFORT SEA
CHUKCHI SEA
BERING SEA
GULF OF ALASKA
PACIFIC OCEAN

ARCTIC CIRCLE
RUSSIA
North Slope
BROOKS RANGE
Gates of the Arctic National Park and Preserve
Kobuk Valley National Park
ALASKA
United States
Yukon
Yukon
Denali National Park and Preserve
Lake Clark National Park and Preserve
Kenai Fjords National Park
Katmai National Park and Preserve
Wrangell-St. Elias National Park and Preserve
Glacier Bay National Park and Preserve
RANGE
CANADA

St. Lawrence Island
Nunivak Island
Kodiak Island

0    150
KILOMETERS
0    150
STATUTE MILES

**HAWAIIAN PARKS**

PACIFIC OCEAN

HAWAI'I
Kaulakahi Chan.
KAUA'I
Ni'ihau
Kaua'i Channel
O'AHU
Pearl Harbor
Kaiwi Channel
MOLOKA'I
MAUI
Haleakalā N.P.
LĀNA'I
Kaho'olawe
'Alenuihāhā Channel
'Upolu Point
HAWAI'I
Hawai'i Volcanoes National Park

0    100
KILOMETERS
0    100
STATUTE MILES

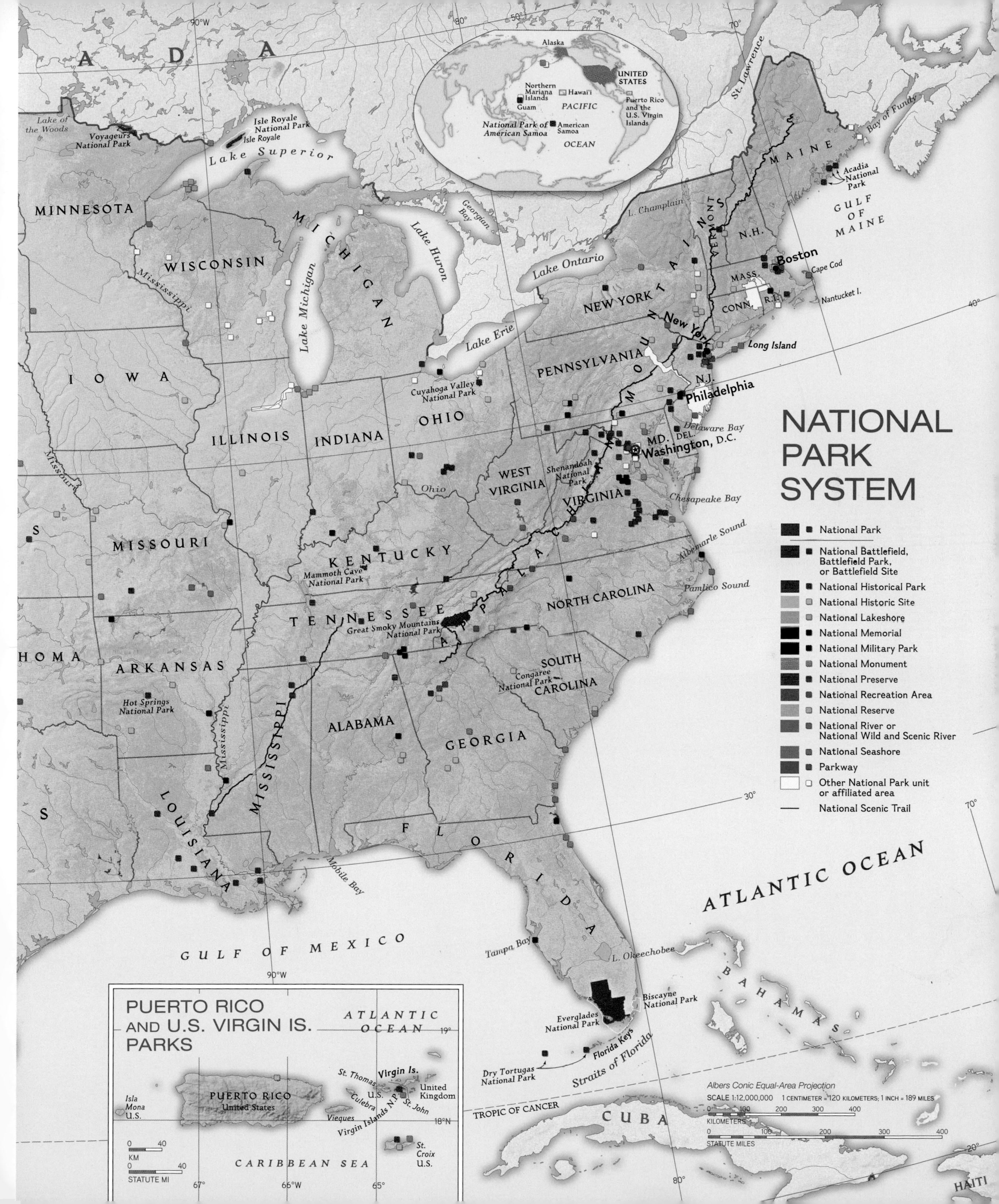
NATIONAL PARK SYSTEM
National Park
National Battlefield, Battlefield Park, or Battlefield Site
National Historical Park
National Historic Site
National Lakeshore
National Memorial
National Military Park
National Monument
National Preserve
National Recreation Area
National Reserve
National River or National Wild and Scenic River
National Seashore
Parkway
Other National Park unit or affiliated area
National Scenic Trail
Alaska
UNITED STATES
Northern Mariana Islands
Hawai'i
Guam
PACIFIC OCEAN
Puerto Rico and the U.S. Virgin Islands
National Park of American Samoa
American Samoa
Voyageurs National Park
Isle Royale National Park
Isle Royale
Lake of the Woods
Lake Superior
MINNESOTA
WISCONSIN
MICHIGAN
Lake Michigan
Lake Huron
Georgian Bay
Lake Ontario
Lake Erie
L. Champlain
St. Lawrence
Bay of Fundy
MAINE
Acadia National Park
GULF OF MAINE
N.H.
VERMONT
MASS.
Boston
Cape Cod
Nantucket I.
CONN.
R.I.
NEW YORK
New York
Long Island
PENNSYLVANIA
N.J.
Philadelphia
Delaware Bay
DEL.
MD.
Washington, D.C.
Chesapeake Bay
IOWA
ILLINOIS
INDIANA
OHIO
Cuyahoga Valley National Park
WEST VIRGINIA
Shenandoah National Park
VIRGINIA
APPALACHIAN MOUNTAINS
Mississippi
Missouri
Ohio
MISSOURI
KENTUCKY
Mammoth Cave National Park
TENNESSEE
Great Smoky Mountains National Park
NORTH CAROLINA
Albemarle Sound
Pamlico Sound
SOUTH CAROLINA
Congaree National Park
ARKANSAS
Hot Springs National Park
HOMA
MISSISSIPPI
ALABAMA
GEORGIA
LOUISIANA
FLORIDA
Mobile Bay
Tampa Bay
L. Okeechobee
Everglades National Park
Biscayne National Park
Dry Tortugas National Park
Florida Keys
Straits of Florida
GULF OF MEXICO
ATLANTIC OCEAN
BAHAMAS
CUBA
HAITI
TROPIC OF CANCER
Albers Conic Equal-Area Projection
SCALE 1:12,000,000 1 CENTIMETER = 120 KILOMETERS; 1 INCH = 189 MILES
KILOMETERS 0 100 200 300 400
STATUTE MILES 0 100 200 300 400
90°W
80°
70°
50°
40°
30°
20°
PUERTO RICO AND U.S. VIRGIN IS. PARKS
ATLANTIC OCEAN
Isla Mona U.S.
PUERTO RICO United States
St. Thomas U.S.
Virgin Is.
United Kingdom
Culebra
Vieques
Virgin Islands N.P.
St. John
St. Croix U.S.
CARIBBEAN SEA
KM 0 40
STATUTE MI 0 40
19°
18°N
67°
66°W
65°

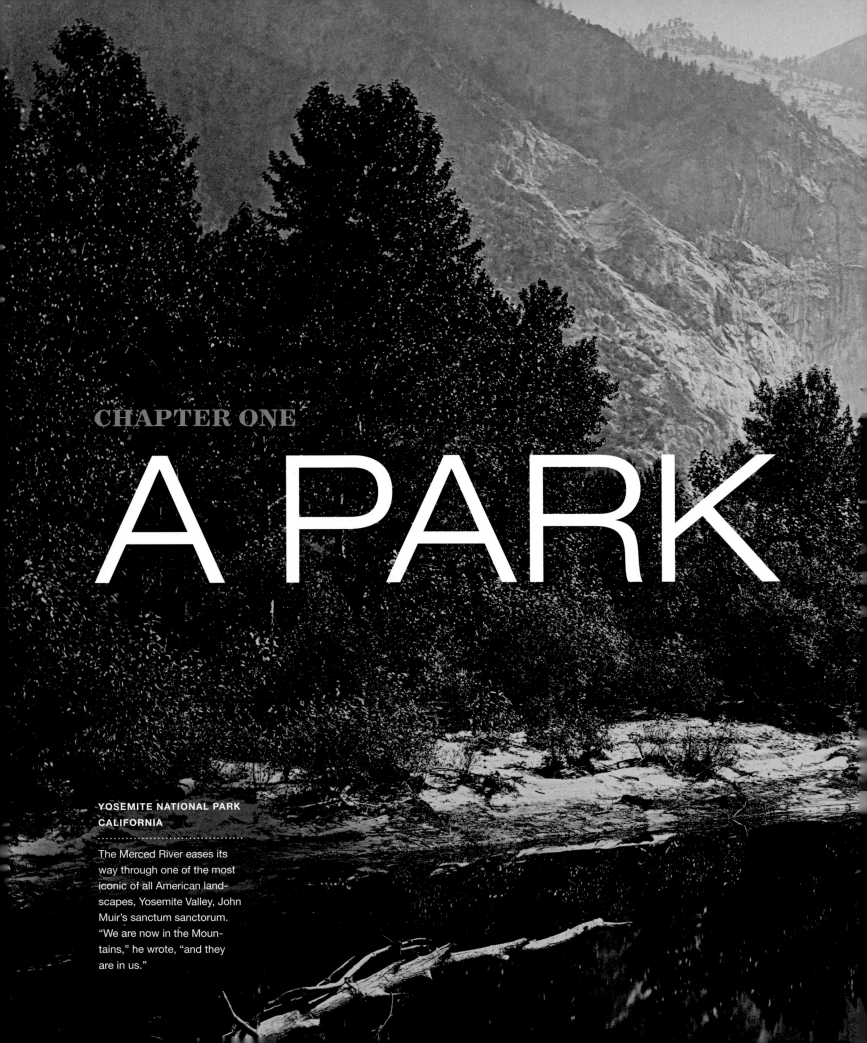

CHAPTER ONE

# A PARK

*is* BORN

# A Park Is Born
## 1803–1916

— ◆◆◆ —

*"The nation behaves well if it treats the natural resources as assets which must be turned over to the next generation increased and not impaired in value."*

### THEODORE ROOSEVELT

How could this happen? Build a dam in a national park? John Muir had fought his last fight. All he could do now, huddled back home in his "scribble den" in December 1913, was wait for Congress to vote, write a few letters to friends, and work on his book on Alaska. He was thin, old, and tired, worn down from many years as the point of the spear of the American conservation movement, standing as he had, largely alone, toe-to-toe with the rapacious juggernauts of the future. His home, which had once seemed so bright with laughter and song, was too big now, too lonely and cold. His wife had died; his two daughters had grown up and moved away.

**YOSEMITE NATIONAL PARK CALIFORNIA**

By the early 1900s, Yosemite National Park, the gem of California, was receiving up to 15,000 visitors per year. While most stayed in Yosemite Valley, a few, such as this man and his dog, climbed high atop the granite peaks for magnificent views of Half Dome and other features.

## HETCH HETCHY
## BEFORE AND AFTER

...................................

"It is hard to bear," John Muir wrote to friends upon receiving the news that his beloved Hetch Hetchy Valley, in Yosemite National Park, would be flooded to provide reliable drinking water and hydroelectric power for the city of San Francisco. The decision galvanized preservationists nationwide and within three years of the Hetch Hetchy decision, the U.S. National Park Service was established.

How could this happen? Build a large dam on a beautiful river and drown a magnificent valley in a national park? In Yosemite, of all places? Dear God.

"Nothing dollarable is safe," Muir once observed.

In the absence of a deep regard for the land, everything becomes a number, a commodity, a utility. Everything is grist to the mill. Trees become board feet. Rivers become gradients and flow volumes.

Where was the outrage? The eloquent dissent?

Where were America's poets, painters, and photographers?

Where was the long reach of the federal government? Not the cold hand of tyranny, but the warm hand of benevolent wisdom that curbed our worst impulses and said, No. Not here. This place we leave alone. As historic preservationist Ann Pamela Cunningham said after a successful career saving Mount Vernon, "Ladies, the Home of Washington is in your charge; see to it that you keep it the Home of Washington. Let no irreverent hand change it; no vandal hands desecrate it with the fingers of progress!"

Did the good people of the United States really want to flood the Hetch Hetchy Valley—a sister to Yosemite Valley, an American Sistine Chapel—to make electricity and a big water impoundment for the city of San Francisco?

If a national park wasn't safe from such industry, what place was?

Muir and other like-minded moralists worried that the vibrant earth, so rich and wondrous and everywhere our daily provider, would one day become our sickly dependent, left to thrive or die at our bidding. We humans who were once small and vulnerable were—with our industry and numbers—making ourselves larger every year.

And yet, we had reason to hope. Why? Because we who could alter any landscape in the world could also choose restraint, the higher ground, to leave a few places as we'd found them, untouched, the apple unpicked.

Amid all our money-getting and town-building, the United States created something unprecedented and profound: a system of national parks. Beginning in that momentous year of 1872, there was just one, Yellowstone, in a territory not yet forged into the states of Wyoming, Montana, and Idaho. Sure, there were state parks—Yosemite, for example. But national parks? Just one. Everybody reasoned, "Yes, we have our park. Now let's get on with the business of business, of transforming the continent and putting it to work." But Yellowstone had power; it had appeal. The reasoning behind its creation—to save a breathing place for the American lungs—was contagious. Europe had its castles and cathedrals; America had its natural wonders, from the mountains to the canyons to the forests to the sea.

And so in time, Yellowstone got its siblings: Yosemite, Sequoia, Mount Rainier, Crater Lake, Mesa Verde, Wind Cave, Zion, and Glacier. Here was something exciting, a uniquely American idea, as original as baseball, as improvisational as jazz, and perhaps as significant as the Constitution itself. Here was something never before tested in the arc of human history, a brake on the wheel, the very thing we might one day need to save us from ourselves, to find out who we were before we got too clever for own good.

OPPOSITE:

**WALNUT DICE | YOSEMITE NATIONAL PARK MUSEUM**

These walnut dice, part of the Yosemite National Park Museum collection, were hand made by Native American Julia Parker. A Coast Miwok/ Kashaya Pomo, Parker is best known for her legendary basket weaving.

**ROOSEVELT AND MUIR YOSEMITE NATIONAL PARK**

"Now this is bully," exclaimed President Teddy Roosevelt after befriending his fellow nature enthusiast, John Muir, during a camping trip on Glacier Point, high above Yosemite Valley, in May 1903.

Captain William Clark used dead reckoning, celestial navigation, a sextant, and a chronometer to make his accurate map, only 40 miles off in an 8,000-mile journey.

The future was out there looking back on us, judging what we did. Asking, how could this happen?

As John Muir wrote, "Thousands of tired, nerve-shaken, over-civilized people are beginning to find out that going to the mountains is going home; that wildness is a necessity; and that mountain parks and reservations are useful not only as fountains of timber and irrigating rivers, but as fountains of life."

How this rediscovery began and continues to this day, and is copied by nations all over the world, is one of the America's greatest and most original ideas.

For more than a century, since the triumphant return of the Lewis and Clark Expedition, and even before, many Americans had dreamed of going west to acquire freedom, land, and wealth. According to historian Stephen Ambrose, Thomas Jefferson, the architect of the Lewis and Clark Expedition, had a mind that "encompassed the continent. From the beginning of the [American] revolution, he thought of the United States as a nation stretching from sea to sea. More than any other man, he made that happen."

Imagine Meriwether Lewis reporting back to Jefferson after more than three years away, the two men in the president's new residence, a building called the Executive Mansion (it would be another full century before Americans called it the White House), spreading out William Clark's field map, hand drawn (we would learn later) to within one half of one percent accuracy. A son of the Enlightenment, Jefferson loved science, accuracy, and detail. "On that point," observed Ambrose, "Lewis had carried out Jefferson's orders exactly . . . How long the debriefing by the commander-in-chief lasted, what subjects came up, what was said, is all conjecture. One fact we do know; they spread the map on the floor, got down on hands and knees, and examined it."

———◆———

IN TRUTH, IT BURDENED Captain Lewis to tell the president that no viable commercial waterway spanned the continent east to west. The Rocky Mountains, among other things, stood in the way. Pulled into the orbit of businessmen in St. Louis, which Ambrose called "that center of get-rich-quick schemes," Lewis, now a national hero, unabashedly sought the handsome profits he'd make one day from a possible fur empire and his published journals, all meticulously written. The great wild continent to the west, while beautiful, he said, was also bountiful, "so liberally bestowed by nature on this fair portion of the globe," and

**LEWIS AND CLARK
PORTRAITS**

No two men were better
suited to lead the Corps
of Discovery than captains
William Clark (left), a tough
woodsman from the Kentucky
frontier, and Meriwether Lewis
(right), a keen natural historian and Thomas Jefferson's
personal secretary. Clark was
also a brilliant surveyor who
made the first map of the
Trans-Mississippi West.

that bounty would prompt Americans "to avail themselves of those resources, to promote the cause of liberty and the honour of America, and to relieve distressed humanity." Whether driven to make profits, to escape poverty, or something in between, no Americans back then—when the continent seemed endless and inexhaustible and in some places downright dangerous—spent their days motivated by large-scale wild lands preservation.

If so, they'd have been considered mad.

Mountains should be tamed in every way possible, forests felled, rivers put to work. Jefferson himself spoke of wild places as "unimproved land." The idea of a national park—and a family vacation to camp in one for pleasure and renewal—was inconceivable.

Amid all this hustle and bustle, where did the first contrarian raise his voice?

------

IRONICALLY, IN EUROPE. About the same time Captain Lewis reported to President Jefferson on his epic achievement, a poet, William Wordsworth, living then in England's Lake District, criticized enterprising man and his blind faith in industry. Having seen coal dust blacken cities, nearby farms, forests, and creeks, and the faces of sickly women and children, he wrote of moral

**YOSEMITE NATIONAL PARK
CALIFORNIA**

..........................................

El Capitan (left) and Bridalveil
Falls (right) captivated those
who viewed them in photo-
graphs like this hand-tinted
black-and-white image by
renowned photographer
Arthur C. Pillsbury.

"impulses" in the woods. "Come forth into the light of things," he said, "let Nature be your teacher." Let it be your hope and salvation. Lord Byron and François-René de Chateaubriand said much the same.

In 1830-31, as Charles Lyell published *Principles of Geology* (with its notion of Earth as being millions—if not billions—of years old) and Charles Darwin departed England to circumnavigate the world on H.M.S. *Beagle,* French aristocrat Alexis de Tocqueville traveled through America and found what he most sought: the frontier, the exciting edge between civilization and the wild. Here, novelist James Fenimore Cooper had shaped his likable protagonist, Natty Bumppo, a man comfortable in both worlds but overall made wise and pure by his time in the woods, uncorrupted—unlike his city

> *"Leave it as it is. You cannot improve on it. The ages have been at work on it, and man can only mar it—keep it for your children, and your children's children, and for all who come after you."*

## PRESIDENT THEODORE ROOSEVELT

*upon first seeing the Grand Canyon*

counterparts. "In Europe people talk a great deal of the wilds of America," Tocqueville wrote, "but the Americans themselves never think about them; they are insensible to the inanimate wonders of nature and they may be said not to perceive the mighty forests that surround them till they fall beneath the hatchet. Their eyes are fixed upon another sight . . . the march across these wild lands, draining swamps, turning the course of rivers, peopling solitudes, and subduing nature."

Yet Americans by the thousands read Wordsworth and English poet Lord Byron. Poets influenced painters as painters influenced poets. Words and images mattered. Back and forth across the Atlantic, moralists such as Ralph Waldo Emerson and Thomas Carlyle exchanged letters on the corrupting influence of industry and machines. Thomas Cole, Asher Durand, and other artists of New York's Hudson River school began to paint landscapes absent of human influence, as if to say, Some places cannot be improved by the hand of man.

*TOP:*
**CRADLEBOARD | SIOUX**

George Catlin wrote that he purchased this cradleboard (made in about 1835) "from a Sioux woman's back, as she was carrying her infant in it . . ." Indian babies were strapped tightly into these carriers, which served as both swaddling and transport.

*OPPOSITE:*
**THE WHITE CLOUD
GEORGE CATLIN**

George Catlin's painting "The White Cloud, Head Chief of the Iowas, 1844/45," a 27-by-22-inch oil on canvas, hangs today in the National Gallery of Art. The Iowa were forced to leave their land by the Indian Removal Act of 1830.

In 1832, artist George Catlin, a native of Pennsylvania, traveled up the
Missouri River and witnessed crazed white men paying Sioux and Mandan
Indians whiskey money to slaughter buffalo. Not for food. Not to make tools.
They slaughtered them for their hides, to make robes, and left the bodies to
rot. Catlin knew that everything he painted was a grand and heartbreaking
evanescence; soon to disappear—forever: the magnificent Indians, the buffalo,
entire cultures and ways of life.

How to save even a piece of it?

He called upon a "great protecting policy of the government" to establish "a
Nation's Park, containing man and beast . . . for America to preserve and hold
up to the view of her refined citizens and the world, in future ages!" The year
before, Tocqueville had made a similar plea for preservation upon seeing the
commercial clutter at Niagara Falls. Despite this, nothing changed. Catlin's
words, like Tocqueville's, were not so much rocks thrown through glass as peb-
bles thrown into a pool. In time, the ripples would travel far and turn to waves.

⟨⟩

SLOWLY, AMERICA CAME TO ITS SENSES.

While daily marching to the drumbeat of material progress, citizens here
and there began to regard wild nature as beneficial, even therapeutic. Congress established Arkansas Hot Springs Reservation in 1832 not for its scenery, but for its medicinal value. A little more than a dozen years later, Henry

David Thoreau walked away from the hustle and bustle of Concord, Massachusetts, and built a cabin on nearby Walden Pond, and for 26 months lived what he called "a sort of border life," to see what he might learn. On a trip to the Maine Woods, he found country "even more grim and wild" than he'd expected—country that made Walden seem tame. It shocked him. "Instead of coming out of the woods with a deepened appreciation of the wild," as historian Roderick Nash wrote, "Thoreau felt a greater respect for civilization and realized the need for balance."

In Boston, Brooklyn, and Philadelphia, citizens hungry for a Sunday respite didn't always attend church. They began to take walks in cemeteries. "If the nation could provide parklands for the dead," historian Alfred Runte would observe, "parklands for the living might also be realized . . . [New York City's] Central Park set a precedent for preservation in the common interest more than a decade before realization of the national park idea." In Virginia in 1858, the Mount Vernon Ladies' Association of the Union, led by the preservationist Louisa Bird Cunningham, acquired George Washington's mansion from his great-grandnephew and rescued it from neglect and disrepair.

Then came the Civil War. "The struggle of today is not altogether for today," President Lincoln told his cabinet. "It is for a vast future also." While referring to his great desire to preserve the union, his words could also apply to slavery and civil rights, and one day, environmental justice—the rights of all citizens to inherit a clean, beautiful, bountiful planet. Lincoln had heard appeals from a small group of Californians about the Mariposa Grove of giant sequoias and

*TOP:*

**SKULL | AMERICAN BISON**

Skulls like this were piled high (and later crushed into fertilizer) in the wake of an unprecedented bison slaughter. Yellowstone National Park offered the besieged animals a refuge.

**SEQUOIA LUMBERJACKS CALIFORNIA**

Lumberjacks pose next to the giant sequoia they've just felled in the early 1900s in what would become Sequoia National Park. "Any fool can destroy trees," John Muir wrote. "They cannot run away; and if they could they would still be destroyed."

# CHACO CANYON

For more than 10,000 years Indians have continuously occupied the Colorado Plateau. The Ancient Pueblo Peoples of Chaco Canyon (in today's northwestern New Mexico) prospered from about A.D. 950 until 1100, and presided over much of the Four Corners region. The canyon is famous for its pottery and architecture. Master builders, the Puebloans employed formal design, astronomical elements, and masonry that enabled them to build the first multiple-story construction in the American Southwest. The largest building, four to five stories high, probably contained more than 600 rooms. Chaco Culture National Historical Park was created as a national monument in 1907, becoming a national historical park in 1980. It was listed as a World Heritage site in 1987. ■

**ARTIFACTS | CHACO CULTURE NATIONAL HISTORICAL PARK, NEW MEXICO**

1. Yucca fiber chain;
2. Argillite bead necklace;
3. Clay vessel fragment;
4. Bone game pieces;
5. Yucca sandal.

⑥

⑦

⑧

⑨

⑩

⑪

**ARTIFACTS | CHACO
CULTURE NATIONAL
HISTORICAL PARK,
NEW MEXICO**

6. Ancestral Puebloan clay
ladle; 7. Trade ware bowl;
8. Turquoise pendant; 9. Trade
ware mug; 10. Bell; 11. Clay
figurines from Pueblo Alto.

a nearby valley called Yosemite: Don't let either become another Niagara Falls. Don't auction them off. We ask that you preserve them "inalienably forever."

In June 1864, while the war dragged on, Lincoln signed the bill into law. The two preserved areas totaled only 44 square miles and made no apologies for incomplete home ranges or watershed boundaries. According to the historian Runte, "Monumentalism, not environmentalism, was the driving impetus behind the 1864 Yosemite Act."

---

PEOPLE IN THE PARKS

# JOHN MUIR

Born in Scotland and raised in Wisconsin, John Muir left home (and his overbearing father) and arrived in California in 1868, one month before his 30th birthday. He hiked fleet-footed through the Sierra Nevada, climbed high peaks, fell in love with Yosemite, and met Ralph Waldo Emerson. Muir detested the timber industry and sheep grazing and began to write in defense of all things wild and free. By 1899, when he finished his seventh and final trip to Alaska, where he practiced what he called his "glacier gospel," he was America's leading preservationist. Muir had a large home in Martinez, where he raised two daughters, but his wild heart always belonged in Yosemite. ∎

EVER SINCE JOHN COLTER struck off from the Lewis and Clark Expedition and walked into the mythical world called Yellowstone, followed in the 1830s by mountain men such as Jim Bridger, fables of geysers and mudpots and bear tracks the size of pie plates had peppered the American imagination. Over many more decades, as railroads spidered west and opened the frontier, rumors (mostly disbelieved) traveled back East. Gold was discovered in Montana in the 1860s; soon Yellowstone's wonders could be confirmed or disclaimed. In September 1869, four months after the completion of the transcontinental railroad (which enabled travel from Boston to San Francisco in less than a week, versus two months spent sailing around Cape Horn), Charles W. Cook, David E. Folsom, and William Peterson rode their horses into Yellowstone and returned with stories of canyons, thermal basins, and rock formations that "bore a strong resemblance of an old castle." Many other "curiosities" of "interest and wonder" caught their attention, including a view of Yellowstone Lake that Folsom called "a scene of transcendent beauty." Of course, other explorers had seen the cliff dwellings of Colorado, the caves of Kentucky, and the mounds of Ohio—and struggled to understand their significance. But this was something else. Cook and Folsom wrote about what they'd seen but had trouble selling the story; it seemed too far-fetched. They finally landed their article in *Western Monthly Magazine* in July 1870, just as a second Yellowstone expedition, composed of 17 men under the commands of Gen. Henry D. Washburn and 2nd Lt. Gustavus C. Doane, made final preparations.

**MAMMOTH HOT SPRINGS | YELLOWSTONE NATIONAL PARK**

..............................

Yellowstone's Mammoth Hot Springs are a geothermal feature in which water flows down a hill of travertine (a kind of limestone). This image was amongst some of the earliest photography of the springs.

*BELOW:*

**TRAVEL BROCHURE | NORTHERN PACIFIC RAILROAD**

..............................

"Wonderland" quickly became a popular description of Yellowstone. The Northern Pacific Railroad used it as a selling point on this 1884 brochure (21" x 9.5"). Featured inside was a letter from a visitor, "Alice in Wonderland."

The Washburn-Doane Expedition of August-September 1870 included the recently appointed territorial governor of Montana, Nathaniel Langford (though he would never fill the post), and a young lawyer and correspondent, the philosophical Cornelius Hedges. It was both a grand adventure—the men like schoolboys, giddy at times, chasing grizzlies and marveling at geysers—and a misadventure, with a head injury, an infected hand, and one member of the party, Truman Everts, gone missing and presumed lost. The thoughtfully poetic names they gave to now famous features—Upper Geyser Basin, Old Faithful, Grand Prismatic Spring, the Castle, the Beehive, the Grotto, and more—stand unchallenged today as enduring symbols of the national park idea.

Such a wonderland. What to do with it? For many decades a sacred "campfire story" persisted—and still does today in some areas—that the men ended their trip sitting around a campfire on a cool September night, sharing ideas. They could build hotels and gift shops at all the most attractive sites and make a lot of money. But Hedges dissented and argued eloquently that the area should be preserved somehow, for everybody in equal share, for the good of all. This was according to Langford, whose 1870 diary from that trip went missing. Many years later, historians Aubrey Haines and Lee Whittlesey argued that the campfire story, while compelling, is almost certainly untrue. From among 17 other journals on that trip, according to Whittlesey, "not one of them corroborated Langford's story of the alleged campfire discussion."

**MOUNT RAINIER NATIONAL
PARK | WASHINGTON**

......................................

This hand-tinted photograph
of the Tatoosh Range in
Mount Rainier National Park
by A. H. Barnes appeared
in the April 1916 issue of
*National Geographic*.

Sacred stories die hard.

According to Langford, whose published accounts of the journey did not appear until 1905, "I lay awake half of last night thinking about it; and if my wakefulness deprived my bedfellow (Hedges) of any sleep, he has only himself and his disturbing national park proposition to answer for it." Perhaps a spirited discussion over the future of Yellowstone took place then between only Langford and Hedges. We will never know.

One thing was certain: The men returned home thin and haggard. According to a witness, all but one appeared unfit to be seen on the street. But when asked about their adventure, the men talked as if they'd discovered a children's fairy tale.

......................................................................................

### "*It will be a park worthy of the great public.*"

### *HELENA HERALD*

*(in support of the Yellowstone National Park idea)*

......................................................................................

Langford arranged with the Northern Pacific Railroad to lecture on Yellowstone throughout the East. In his Washington audience that winter was Ferdinand V. Hayden, director of the U.S. Geological and Geographical Survey of the Territories.

**APACHE BASKET**
**JOHN MUIR COLLECTION**

.........................................

On display at John Muir National Historic Site, at his home in Martinez, California, where he lived from 1880 until 1914, is an Apache or Yavapai basket, made of split willow shoots.

THE FOLLOWING SUMMER, Hayden led a large investigative expedition into the territorial region, complete with zoologists, entomologists, mineralogists, the artist Thomas Moran (who was subsidized by Northern Pacific), and landscape photographer William Henry Jackson. Hayden's 1871 expedition confirmed nearly all reports that had come before. He and his men found Mammoth Hot Springs, which the previous two expeditions had missed, and returned back East with an unembellished pictorial record. "There is something romantic in the thought," effused the *New York Times,* "that, in spite of the restless activity of our people, and the almost fabulous rapidity of their increase, vast tracts of national domain yet remain unexplored."

Yellowstone quickly became the darling of the popular press, and the talk of Congress and the nation. Moran's stunning 7-by-12-foot canvas painting,

*Grand Canyon of the Yellowstone,* was purchased by Congress for $10,000 and featured in the U.S. Senate lobby. Hayden spoke publicly on the nation's failure to protect Niagara Falls from crass commercialism. Here was a chance to do things right, he said, to preserve antiquity on a whole new scale, where sights "more beautiful than human art ever conceived . . . ought to be as free as the air and water." Unsuitable for mining, farming, or timbering, the Yellowstone region had another calling. Its greatest gifts—scenic wonder and beauty—should be forever preserved in a *national park.*

Bills moved quickly through the House and Senate, and on March 1, 1872, President Ulysses S. Grant signed the Yellowstone Park Act into law. The world would never again be quite the same.

The protection President Lincoln afforded to California's Yosemite and the surrounding area, while masterful in 1864, seemed insufficient when compared with that of Yellowstone in 1872, and John Muir knew it. Men he called "timber thieves" and domestic sheep he called "hoofed locusts" were decimating the Sierra. Private inholdings popped up everywhere like weeds. Magnificent trees, many of them thousands of years old, were felled as if they were matchsticks. When Robert Underwood Johnson, an influential editor, offered Muir the chance to write back-to-back magazine articles on the imperiled beauty of Yosemite and the Sierra, Muir said yes. Again, the timing was perfect. Letters

**YELLOWSTONE**
**THOMAS MORAN**

. . . . . . . . . . . . . . . . . . . . . . . . . . . . . . . . . . . . . . .

Thomas Moran's painting of the so-called Lower Yellowstone Range typifies his genius for rendering landscapes with great depth and tone, and little or no exaggeration. His Yellowstone work, inspired during the 1871 Hayden expedition, put him on a par with America's other great western landscape painter, Albert Bierstadt, of Yosemite fame.

flooded into Congress. On October 1, 1890, we had three new national parks: Sequoia, General Grant, and Yosemite (though Yosemite Valley remained—until 1905—under California state jurisdiction).

Back East, military history enthusiasts worked hard to preserve the hallowed grounds of many Civil War battlefield sites, and were succeeding.

By the turn of the century, according to Alfred Runte, "the first glimmerings of a national park system had begun to emerge; still unresolved was how long and how well the nation would be committed to maintaining it." In 1899, after five years of political struggle, during which preservationists had to convince Congress that no valuable forests would be closed to the timber industry, Mount Rainier National Park was finally established as the first national park in the Pacific Northwest; it was also the first carved from a forest reserve. Crater Lake followed in 1903.

That same year President Theodore Roosevelt made a grand tour (by train) of the western states. He visited Yellowstone and the Grand Canyon (not yet a national park), and he camped in Yosemite with John Muir. Enthused by each other's company, the two naturalists told stories late into the night and shared their heartfelt desires to protect wild lands. What Roosevelt needed was a tool to establish a protected area without the consent of Congress. He got it in 1906 with passage of the American Antiquities Act. Intended to protect small archaeological sites from vandalism, the act—called by some "the greatest piece of conservation legislation nobody's ever heard of"—permitted the president to quickly create a national monument from federal land by executive order, with the stroke of a pen. Roosevelt took it and ran with it. First came Devils Tower National Monument, followed by El Morro, Montezuma Castle, Tonto, Gila Cliff Dwellings, Muir Woods, Jewel Cave, Natural Bridges, Petrified Forest, Pinnacles, Grand Canyon, Mount Olympus, and others. Of the 18 national monuments established by Teddy Roosevelt in three years, many later became national parks. And all soon became units within the National Park System, administered by the National Park Service.

.......................................

Wizard Island, in the center of the image, at Oregon's spectacular Crater Lake

PEOPLE IN THE PARKS

# TEDDY ROOSEVELT

Twenty years younger than John Muir, Teddy Roosevelt was the first U.S. president born and raised in New York City. Despite this, he loved the West, and the plains, and what he called "the strenuous life." Beware long hours in the soft sofa and padded chair, he said. Get out there. Sleep on the ground. Eat wild game. America had never had such a president. A self-described "Audubonist" and nature lover, Roosevelt was also a trustbuster, with few friends on Wall Street. And he didn't care. From 1903 to 1908, he established 230 million acres of preserved public lands (including 18 national monuments and five national parks)—an area larger than Texas and California combined. ∎

Again and again the banner to establish a new national park was carried by a few—if not just one or two—committed citizens sustained by vision, courage, and patient persistence. William Gladstone Steel had championed Crater Lake ever since, as a child, he had seen a photo of the lake in a newspaper wrapped around his school-lunch sandwich. George Bird Grinnell, the editor of *Forest and Stream* and the co-founder, with Teddy Roosevelt, of the Boone and Crockett Club (dedicated to wildlife conservation), led the charge for Glacier National Park, in northwest Montana. And Enos Mills, after a life-changing encounter with John Muir, devoted himself to the creation of Colorado's Rocky Mountain National Park.

Of course, as with all noble causes, there were setbacks. In the aftermath of a devastating earthquake that left 400,000 people homeless and without a reliable source of good drinking water, the city of San Francisco lobbied vigorously to dam the Tuolumne River and flood Hetch Hetchy Valley in Yosemite National Park. Pitting aesthetics against practicality, the debate split the Sierra Club and made enemies of friends. It drew national attention and forced Americans to ask: What's a national park for? The bill finally passed Congress and was signed by President Woodrow Wilson in December 1913. Some said it broke John Muir's heart. He died one year later.

———◈———

HOW COULD THIS HAPPEN? "the most significant thing about the controversy . . . was that it occurred at all," Roderick Nash wrote in 1967.

"One hundred or even fifty years earlier a similar proposal to dam a wilderness river would not have occasioned the slightest ripple of public protest." But while Hetch Hetchy was an end, it was also a beginning. Runte observes, "No defeat so forced the issue of how best to guard the national parks in an urban, industrial age." Preservationists said the national parks and monuments would one day attract large crowds and pay for themselves, but only if they were properly safeguarded. They needed to be managed within their own agency, rather than by whatever bureau had controlled the land prior to its receiving national park or national monument status. Mount Olympus National Monument, for example, managed by the Forest Service, was slashed in half to accommodate the timber industry. This had to stop. "The present situation in regard to the national parks [and monuments] is very bad," said Frederick Law Olmstead, Jr., son of the co-creator of Central Park. He and others called for a new federal agency to protect the parks in perpetuity, for the enjoyment of all. This was no easy task.

   In 1915, more than 100,000 people visited America's national parks. By early 1916, two men, one wealthy, one poor, were positioned to lead that agency— and the parks—into a whole new era. ∎

**LONGS PEAK | ROCKY MOUNTAIN NATIONAL PARK**

An early image shows hikers looking out over Longs Peak in Rocky Mountain National Park. Stephen T. Mather described Rocky Mountain National Park as "glorious" during the park's dedication ceremony in 1915.

# THE FIRST PARKS

## 1803–1916

"HITCH YOUR WAGON to a star," Ralph Waldo Emerson wrote, inciting people to dream big and achieve greatness. America did precisely that with its national parks, beginning with Yellowstone, Yosemite, and Sequoia and expanding from there, creating a universe unto itself. Soon magical constellations of parks, most out West, began to appear on the maps of the United States. They colored our imagination and inspired us to conserve, learn, and explore. Europe had its castles and museums; America had its parks, each a unique investment—in the past, present, and future— that belonged to no one and everyone.

**NATURAL BRIDGES
NATIONAL MONUMENT | UTAH**

·····································

Located in southeast Utah,
Natural Bridges National
Monument was established
by President Theodore Roosevelt to protect the many
delicate sedimentary rock
arches that at times appear
to float in the heavens.

# YELLOWSTONE

DAWN SILHOUETTES a crenellated tower. Vapor rises from its center like an early-morning cook fire. Then, with an explosion, water shoots 90 feet into the air and plays erratically for 20 minutes, followed by an hour's display of billowing steam that almost obscures the risen sun. Slowly the exhibition ends and Castle Geyser sleeps again.

Nearby, 370-foot-wide Grand Prismatic Spring steams incessantly at a temperature near 150° F. The blue-green spring wears a raveled collar of yellow, red, and brown algae in this eagle's-eye view. An empty boardwalk rimming the pool is the only mark of man's presence.

"Ageless Splendors of Our Oldest National Park,"
*National Geographic,* May 1972

**YELLOWSTONE NATIONAL PARK | WYOMING**

This aerial view shows the largest hot spring in Yellowstone, Grand Prismatic Spring, which measures 370 feet wide and is more than 121 feet deep. The center of the pool, where water boils up from below, is sterile and too hot to support life; it remains a deep blue year-round. Elsewhere, pigmented bacteria render a kaleidoscope of colors that vary through the seasons as the different bacteria thrive and die in the mineral-rich water. Visitors are cautioned: Look, but don't touch.

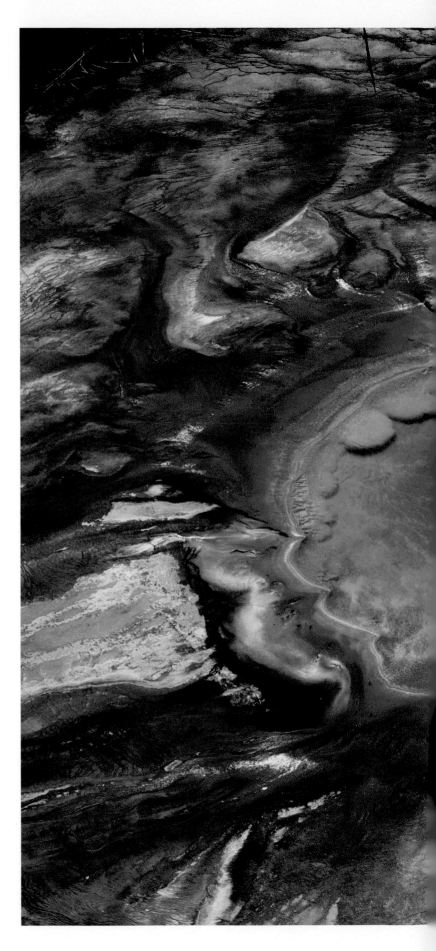

*"Writing of an 1889 hunting trip in Idaho, my great-great-grandfather described 'a half melancholy feeling as I gazed on these bison, themselves part of the last remnant of a doomed and nearly vanished race. Few, indeed, are the men who now have, or evermore shall have, the chance of seeing the mightiest of American beasts.' "*

**TED ROOSEVELT V**

*great-great-grandson of President Theodore Roosevelt*

**YELLOWSTONE NATIONAL PARK | WYOMING**

A bison covered in ice rests on the ground in Yellowstone. Yellowstone National Park—established to preserve natural scenery, not wildlife—became a refuge to the North American bison after more than 60 million were reduced to fewer than 1,000.

SEQUOIA NATIONAL
PARK | CALIFORNIA

In this park's 400,000 acres
in the southern Sierra
Nevada, visitors can admire
the passage of centuries as
measured by Tokopah Falls
(above) and giant sequoias
(above right). Among the
giants is the General Sherman
Tree (opposite), one of the
largest trees on Earth. It can
be reached by an easy 0.8-
mile loop trail that takes hikers past five of the ten largest
trees in the world.

FROM THE ARCHIVES

# THE GIANT SEQUOIAS

ON A GENTLE SLOPE ABOVE A TRAIL junction in Sequoia National Park, about 7,000 feet above sea level in the southern Sierra Nevada, looms a very big tree. Its trunk is rusty red, thickened with deep layers of furrowed bark, and 27 feet in diameter at the base. Its footprint would cover your dining room. Trying to glimpse its tippy top, or craning to see the shape of its crown, could give you a sore neck. That is, this tree is so big you can scarcely look at it all. It has a name, the President, bestowed about 90 years ago by admiring humans. It's a giant sequoia, a member of *Sequoiadendron giganteum,* one of several surviving species of redwoods.

It's not quite the largest tree on Earth. It's the second largest. Recent research by scientist Steve Sillett of Humboldt State University and his colleagues has confirmed that the President ranks number two among all big trees that have ever been measured—and Sillett's team has measured quite a few.

David Quammen, "Forest Giant," *National Geographic,* December 2012

# YOSEMITE LIFE

THE PICTURE THAT MANY PEOPLE have of this lovely 1,189-square-mile park in California's Sierra Nevada as jammed from end to end with people and cars just isn't true. I know Yosemite well. I've been visiting it for years, and last summer I roamed all over it. There is congestion, but only in places.

If a man finds joy in crowds and wants comforts, he goes to Yosemite Valley, or to Tuolumne Meadows along Tioga Road. But if he wants to be alone, he need only step off the beaten path. A whopping 90 percent of Yosemite is roadless wilderness in which he might not see another soul for days.

Variety is Yosemite's strong suit. This park lets a man hike, fish, swim, square dance, ride a horse, camp in a tent or in a motor home with chrome trim. He can watch 220 kinds of birds, hobnob with bears (careful!), drive a pack burro, ride a bike, slide down a glacier, live in a deluxe hotel, study 1,400 kinds of wild flowers.

Nathaniel T. Kenney, "The Other Yosemite,"
*National Geographic,* June 1974

**YOSEMITE NATIONAL PARK | CALIFORNIA**

A male mule deer feeds on a milkweed plant, backlit in Cook's Meadow. Early visitors to the national parks, most of them from towns and cities, enjoyed seeing deer and other ungulates. They found predators frightful, however. So the U.S. Army, and later the National Park Service, began culling predators to make deer and elk more plentiful and easy to see. Stephen T. Mather, the first director of the National Park Service, supported predator control and reported a "very gratifying increase in deer and other species that always suffer through the depredations of mountain lion, wolves, and other 'killers.'" In time, the Park Service ceased its predator-control programs and matured into the ecology-minded agency it is today.

*"But no temple made with hands
can compare with Yosemite.
Every rock in its walls seems to glow with life."*
**JOHN MUIR**

# MOUNT RAINIER: THEN & NOW

IF ALL GOES WELL, we will be high on Everest by the time you read this article. Our best energies will be aimed at becoming the first Americans, and the third party in history, to scale this monarch of all mountains. We will also attempt its sister peaks, Lhotse and Nuptse. And our ultimate success will hinge in part on how well we did our homework on Mount Rainier last summer.

And why, you may wonder, did we choose Rainier, that picture postcard peak within an easy two-hour drive of Tacoma or Seattle? What does this often-climbed, 14,410-foot landmark have in common with the breathless heights of near-inaccessible Everest?

Snow, for one thing—more than 83 feet a record season, piling up drifts deep enough to bury a three-story house, hurtling down in avalanches that can sweep a man away from sight and rescue.

Glaciers, for another—26 of them, and most found on any single mountain in the United States.

And finally, fickle weather—the kind that can beset climbers with chilling fog, hot sun, and blinding blizzard—and all in the space of a few hours.

More than a mountaineering venture, however, the Everest Expedition is making intensive scientific studies supported by the National Geographic Society, the State Department Bureau of Educational and Cultural Affairs, the National Science Foundation, the Office of Naval Research, the Air Force Office of Scientific Research, the Army Quartermaster Research and Engineering Center, and others. On Rainier, we completed plans for these studies, ranging from the growth of glaciers to the psychological reactions of an exhausted climber.

Barry C. Bishop, "Mount Rainier: Testing Ground for Everest,"
*National Geographic,* May 1963

1920

**MOUNT RAINIER NATIONAL PARK | WASHINGTON**

John Muir climbed it in 1888 and afterward lobbied for its protection. Unless the surrounding lowlands are protected, "the flower bloom will soon be killed, and nothing of the forests will be left but black stump monuments."

*"Imagine a vast mountain six by seven miles through, at an elevation of eight thousand feet, with the top removed and the inside hollowed out, then filled with the clearest water in the world . . . And you have a perfect representation of Crater Lake."*

## WILLIAM GLADSTONE STEEL

**CRATER LAKE NATIONAL PARK | OREGON**

When Mount Mazama erupted 7,700 years ago, the top third of the volcano blew off. Slowly the crater filled with rainfall and snowmelt, and a lake was born, 1,943 feet deep—the deepest lake in the United States. Crater Lake became the nation's sixth national park.

## CHICKASAW NATIONAL RECREATION AREA | OKLAHOMA

.........................................................................

Another landmark in American conservation was achieved when
the federal government, in cooperation with two Indian nations,
the Chickasaw and Choctaw, established Platt National Park (1902)
from Sulphur Springs Reservation. Today, as Chickasaw National
Recreation Area, it offers many of the same activities visitors
enjoyed in the early 1900s.

*OPPOSITE:*

## WIND CAVE NATIONAL PARK | SOUTH DAKOTA

.........................................................................

Wind Cave offers two worlds of subtle beauty. Aboveground lies one of
America's few remaining intact prairies while belowground visitors can
see one of the world's longest caves. Throughout the 1920s, Stephen
T. Mather, the National Park Service's first director, promoted the
hiring of what he called "ranger naturalists" to help improve the
Park Service's image of friendly professionalism. It worked.

# MESA VERDE

DEEP IN COLORADO'S SOUTHWEST corner, high among the cliffs of majestic Mesa Verde, Indian chant and laughter echoed for 1,300 years—then died in a series of drought-stricken seasons two centuries before Columbus. Mountain lion and mule deer fell heir to a lonely realm of fortresslike dwellings and strange ceremonial kivas.

Now, on Wetherill Mesa—a remote and hitherto undeveloped area of Mesa Verde National Park—the National Park Service and the National Geographic Society have launched a major archeological project which will shed new light on these shadowy pre-historic builders. Eventually it will open an imposing series of little-known, long-silent cliff dwellings to the American people.

"Mesa Verde has one of the largest concentrations of prehistoric ruins in the United States," says Conrad L. Wirth, Director of the National Park Service and a Trustee of The Society. "Of its hundreds of known archeological sites, only a few have been scientifically excavated and opened to public inspection."

"Your Society to Seek New Light on the Cliff Dwellers,"
*National Geographic,* January 1959

**MESA VERDE NATIONAL PARK | COLORADO**

Established in 1906 as the first national park to "preserve the works of man," Mesa Verde opened a new and exciting chapter in the history of American conservation. For more than 700 years (roughly from A.D. 600 to 1300), the ancestral Puebloan people lived here. Today the park preserves more than 600 cliff dwellings and 5,000 known archaeological sites.

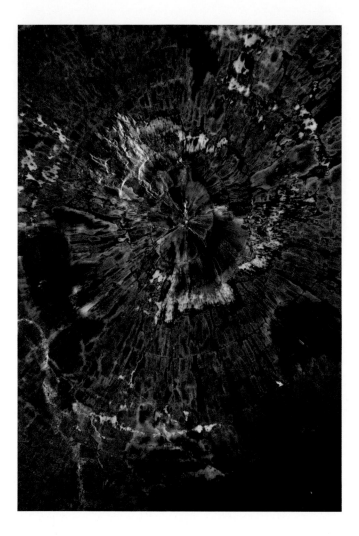

**PETRIFIED FOREST NATIONAL PARK | ARIZONA**

In his later years, as he suffered through heartbreak and the pains
of aging, John Muir found great comfort in Arizona's Petrified
Forest. He loved the clear nights, starry skies, warm days, and, of
course, the fragile grasslands and pieces of late Triassic petrified
wood everywhere, looking like bright constellations on the ground.
Established as a national monument by his friend President Teddy
Roosevelt in 1906, the year after Muir's wife died, Petrified Forest
is today a national park, and it still offers the magic that John Muir
received more than a century ago.

# JOHN MUIR'S LIVING LEGACY

NOTHING QUITE SO ENTRANCED Muir's imagination as trees—trees of any sort, particularly during a storm. Once, when a windstorm erupted while he was exploring the Yuba River Valley, he climbed to the madly swaying top of a Douglas fir and "clung with muscles firm braced, like a bobolink on a reed," remaining there for hours to hear the needles chorusing in the wind.

He often demonstrated this capacity for transmuting physical danger into a kind of spiritual ecstasy. While climbing a canyon wall above Yosemite one day, he heard a terrible roar and abruptly found himself riding a snow avalanche 2,500 feet down to the canyon floor.

Landing miraculously unhurt, he exulted in "This flight in what might be called a milky way of snow-stars . . . the most spiritual and exhilarating of all the modes of motion I have ever experienced. Elijah's flight in a chariot of fire could hardly have been more gloriously exciting."

Harvey Arden, "John Muir's Wild America,"
*National Geographic,* April 1973

**MUIR WOODS NATIONAL MONUMENT | CALIFORNIA**

In the first decade of the 1900s, John Muir stood alone as America's premier defender of wild places and all living things. He especially loved trees, and was 70 years old when he discovered that William and Elizabeth Kent were naming and preserving a forest of magnificent coastal redwoods in his honor. "This is the best tree-lovers monument that could ever be found in all the forests of the world," Muir exclaimed. Located in Marin County, just north of San Francisco, Muir Woods is today a world of green verticality; an island of calm in a large metropolitan area that contains seven million people.

# THE KINO MISSION: THEN & NOW

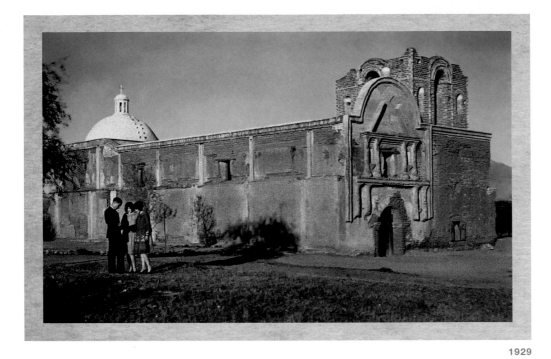

**1929**

**TUMACÁCORI
NATIONAL HISTORICAL
PARK | ARIZONA**

Jesuit padre Eusebio Francisco Kino came to the New World in 1681 and established a Sonora chain of 24 missions in 24 years—the Kino missions—including the mission church of Tumacácori (south of present-day Tucson, Arizona) in 1691. This more recent *National Geographic* photo (opposite) captures the mission accompanied by California poppies, brightly sunlit in what John Muir would regard as the Church of Nature.

NO TWO CITIES ON OUR CONTINENT have been more widely separated than Phoenix and Salt Lake. Now, north and south, from Salt Lake to the Mexican border, another great channel is open to tourist traffic, and increasing thousands will use it.

The astonishing story of prehistoric man in Arizona is graphically revealed in the University Museum at Tucson.

On view there are the actual clothing, implements, utensils, weapons, and jewelry used by cliff dwellers and other forgotten people.

In her treasure-hunting, Indian-fighting, wild-oats age, Arizona took no thought of archeology. She dug for gold, not for bones, beads, or broken pots. Now it is different. She has grown conscious, and proud. So she repairs and restores the cliff dwellings and the *casas grandes,* and archeologists who delve into her ruins are no longer permitted to ship all their finds to museums back East.

"We are grateful for aid in the study of our amazing archeology," said one Arizonian, "and we are willing to divide our excavated relics of antiquity with those from the East, but unless we check their speed a bit the day will come when there won't be a skeleton, a stone ax, or prehistoric bean pot left in the State."

Frederick Simpich, "Arizona Comes of Age," *National Geographic,* January 1929

*"If this destruction of the cliff-houses of New Mexico, Colorado and Arizona goes on at the same rate in the next fifty years that it has in the past, these unique dwellings will be practically destroyed."*

## JESSE WALTER FEWKES

*Anthropologist, August 1896*

### NAVAJO NATIONAL MONUMENT | ARIZONA

Nestled below sandstone alcoves, the three cliff dwellings at Navajo National Monument in northeast Arizona date from around A.D. 1250 to 1300. The Ancestral Puebloans farmed the canyons and hunted wild animals, as well as grew beans, corn, and squash. This particular dwelling, called Keet Seel, is composed of sandstone, mud, mortar, and wood, and remains largely unchanged from when it was occupied.

# THE NARROWS OF ZION

"LET'S GO THROUGH THE NARROWS of the Virgin River this summer," wrote my brother Nate. He enclosed photographs which he had made on a brief scouting trip earlier in the year. His letter breathed enthusiasm.

We had long dreamed of such a trip into the wilds of southwestern Utah's Zion National Park. Here the North Fork of the Virgin River has been chief actor in one of those geological dramas which were responsible for so many of our country's miracles-in-stone.

Eons ago, when the land started to rise from the sea, a stream meandered gently southward. As the land rose, the stream cut slowly but inevitably into the underlying rocks. Like an endless belt of sandpaper, grit-bearing water scoured its way through layer after layer of sandstone until it dug a fantastic, sheer-walled canyon.

Today, with a fall 10 times that of the Colorado in Grand Canyon National Park, the Virgin River tumbles along a channel that reaches a depth of 2,000 feet; at the bottom it is little wider than many a city street.

Lewis F. Clark, "Amid the Mighty Walls of Zion,"
*National Geographic,* January 1954

**ZION NATIONAL PARK | UTAH**

...........................................................

"There will always be one more river," wrote Edward Abbey, "not to cross but to follow." The Virgin River of Zion—Utah's first national park—invites hikers to get their feet wet. Transiting the Narrows, there is no trail. High sandstone walls enclose a river corridor that in some places is only 20 feet wide. "Close-toed shoes and a hiking stick are recommended," says the National Park Service. And don't forget a sense of adventure.

## SALINAS PUEBLO MISSIONS NATIONAL
## MONUMENT | NEW MEXICO

. . . . . . . . . . . . . . . . . . . . . . . . . . . . . . . . . . . . . . . . . . . . . . . . . . . . . .

The ruins of three mission churches are all that remain of what was
a thriving community of Puebloan Indians and Spanish Franciscan
missionaries in the early 1600s. First established as Gran Quivira
National Monument in 1909, the site was enlarged in 1980 and
1981, and given its present name in 1988.

*OPPOSITE:*

## SITKA NATIONAL HISTORICAL PARK | ALASKA

. . . . . . . . . . . . . . . . . . . . . . . . . . . . . . . . . . . . . . . . . . . . . . . . . . . . . .

Totem poles stand a quiet vigil in Sitka, where in 1804 Tlingit Indians
battled Russian fur traders who had invaded their centuries-old
homeland to harvest valuable sea otters pelts. After a six-day siege,
the Tlingit retreated and didn't return until 1821, at the behest of the
Russians, who, the National Park Service says, "intended to profit
off the Indians' hunting expertise." Russia sold Alaska to the United
States in 1867.

**GLACIER NATIONAL PARK | MONTANA**

Stunning dramatic light breaks through stormy skies onto waves pounding the shore of Saint Mary Lake. This park has more than 700 miles of hiking trails and forms an international park with Canada's Waterton Lakes National Park immediately to the north.

# GLACIER NATIONAL PARK

THAT AFTERNOON AS CLOUDS CONTINUED to pile up over the mountains, the dark-bellied sky crackled with jagged light and Thunder strode back into the land. He had been away since fall, and to celebrate his return—for who but this mighty sky spirit sends rains to make the berries full and the sweet grasses tall across the plains—the Blackfeet always opened the medicine pipe bundle. As the hides of elk and grizzly bear were unwrapped, many songs were sung. Berries were ceremonially planted, and a flute called the birds back into the country.

As today, the loons were always among the first to arrive, followed by the meadowlarks, and then the grebes, mergansers, swallows, and their hunters, bald eagles and falcons. The bundle is still opened each spring, and the songs are still sung, though not as many know the words now.

Douglas H. Chadwick, "Spring Comes Late to Glacier,"
*National Geographic,* July 1979

**PINNACLES NATIONAL PARK | CALIFORNIA**

. . . . . . . . . . . . . . . . . . . . . . . . . . . . . . . . . . . . . . . . . . . . . . . . . . . . . . . . .

For many units within the National Park Service, protective designations come in increments. Although Pinnacles was established as a national monument by President Teddy Roosevelt in 1908, not until 1976, 12 years after the passage of the 1964 Wilderness Act, did portions of the monument (together with a dozen other national parks and monuments) receive designation as federally protected wilderness. Finally, in 2013, President Barack Obama signed legislation changing its designation from "monument" to "park." Sights within the park include the eerily spectacular California condor (above) and rock formations (right).

**DINOSAUR NATIONAL MONUMENT | UTAH**

. . . . . . . . . . . . . . . . . . . . . . . . . . . . . . . . . . . . . . . . . . . . . .

A technician perches on a cliff face to outline dinosaur fossil
bones. After Earl Douglass, a paleontologist working for the
Carnegie Museum of Natural History, discovered this site in 1909
and shipped thousands of fossils back East, President Woodrow
Wilson established Dinosaur National Monument to keep the
fossils on-site.

*OPPOSITE:*

**ROCKY MOUNTAIN NATIONAL PARK | COLORADO**

. . . . . . . . . . . . . . . . . . . . . . . . . . . . . . . . . . . . . . . . . . . . . .

Straddling the Continental Divide, this 265,000-acre park contains
72 peaks over 12,000 feet in elevation, with nearly one-fourth of the
park above tree line. In 1884 a 14-year-old boy, Enos Mills, moved
to Estes Park, fell in love with the Front Range Rockies, and after a
chance meeting with John Muir, dedicated much of his adult life to
the establishment of this park. His dream came true in 1915, seven
years before his death.

# ACADIA NATIONAL PARK

THE TWO OF US GO BACK a long way, Acadia and I, half a century and then some. She scared me half to death that first time out—me, the vertiginous flatlander recklessly flouting acute acrophobia one foggy morning on the park's most precipitous trail. Then, on safer ground, she seduced me with her variegated forests and glimmering ponds and surf-splashed headlands, and I found myself, over the years, going back to search out her secret places and scenic vistas again and again. She'll hook you too, if you give her a chance. And watch yourself, in particular, if you should happen that way when autumnal incandescence begins to glow across the domed ridges and U-shaped valleys of Acadia National Park. You like fall foliage, Yankee style? Acadia deals a royal flush almost every time.

Anchored on Maine's Mount Desert Island, a bit under 200 air miles northeast of Boston, Acadia, at some 47,000 acres, is one of the smallest of the national parks but ranks among the most visited.

John G. Mitchell, "Autumn in Acadia National Park,"
*National Geographic,* November 2005

**ACADIA NATIONAL PARK | MAINE**

. . . . . . . . . . . . . . . . . . . . . . . . . . . . . . . . . . . . . . . . . . . . . . . . . . . .

The oldest national park east of the Mississippi River, Acadia preserves much of Maine's Mount Desert Island (including Cadillac Mountain—the tallest mountain on the U.S. Atlantic coast) and other nearby smaller islands. The creation of this park (called Lafayette National Park until 1929) required great vision, determination, and philanthropy on the part of landscape architect Charles Eliot, and his father, the president of Harvard University, Charles W. Eliot, plus George B. Dorr, the "father of Acadia National Park," and John D. Rockefeller, Jr., among others.

*"Our idea as to the park has been to develop it for . . .
people who would be responsive to the beauty
and inspiration of its scenery, and can get away
for a brief or longer holiday."*

**GEORGE B. DORR**
*the "father of Acadia National Park"*

An aerial view reveals morning sunlight slicing through thick fog and the autumn-burnished canopy of a mixed hardwood-evergreen forest. This park contains more than 120 miles of hiking trails, many of them, says the National Park Service, "established by village improvement societies in the late 1800s and early 1900s. Today many of the historical features, such as stonework, are still visible." Acadia's colorful scenery is complemented by an equally colorful human history.

## FROM THE ARCHIVES

# HAWAII VOLCANOES

FOUNTAINING OUT OF THE VENT, the monstrous wave oozed through a forest of ohia trees on Hawaii. Burned off at the base 100 footers toppled like matchsticks. As the mass crossed the road, it sent this tentacle down the straightway at 500 feet an hour. Clinkers rode the crest until they tumbled off the front edge and then, like the treads of a caterpillar tractor, paved a way for the hot, mobile core.

"At this point," writes photographer [Jerry P.] Eaton, "we could hear the dull roar of the fountain half a mile away, the crackling brush burning at the edge of the flow, the glassy tinkle and clatter of clinkers rolling down the front. The odor was smoke; the sensation, heat; the emotion, awe."

Paul A. Zahl, Ph.D., "Volcanic Fires of the 50th State,"
*National Geographic,* June 1959

**HAWAII VOLCANOES NATIONAL PARK | HAWAII**

A mongoose eats a nene (above), Hawaii's endangered state bird—found nowhere else in the world. Farmers created ecological havoc when they introduced the mongoose from Jamaica in 1883 to rid their sugarcane fields of rats. On the flank of Kilauea, one of the world's most active volcanoes, the remote vent Pu'u 'O'o (left) shoots molten lava from a 25-foot-high spatter cone as it surges to life at dusk, on the Big Island of Hawaii.

## FROM THE ARCHIVES

# LASSEN VOLCANIC NATIONAL PARK

DUNES OF ASH, tinted yellow and red from minerals, drift from the cone, a Martian landscape colonized by a few stunted pines.

It's a much abused country. Forest fires, fortified by too much brush and tinder, often sear the land on top; fire and brimstone rise like demons from below.

Near the top of Mount Shasta, 70 miles northwest of Lassen, a thermal field vents sulfurous fumes. Thousands of climbers scale the peak in summer months. "The stuff has a pH of approximately 2," said Michael Zanger, a mountaineer from the town of Mt. Shasta. "It would eat the chrome right off your camera."

Priit J. Vesilind, "ONCE AND FUTURE FURY: California's Volcanic North,"
*National Geographic,* October 2001

**LASSEN VOLCANIC NATIONAL PARK**
**CALIFORNIA**

......................................

Visitors to Lassen Volcanic National Park's Devil's Kitchen (opposite) find themselves in a netherworld of creation and destruction, where steam vents into the crisp, clear, high-elevation air. A volcanic hydrothermal feature lies at the trees' edge in the section of the park known as Bumpass Hell (above).

**LASSEN VOLCANIC NATIONAL PARK | CALIFORNIA**

Lassen Volcanic National Park is a strong example of a place that was originally established as a park to protect its scenic and geologic wonders but over time has proved equally valuable as a refuge for biodiversity. It's a land where three great biological provinces come together—the Cascade Range from the north, the Sierra Nevada from the south, and the Great Basin Desert from the east—and home to more than 700 species of flowering plants and 250 species of vertebrates.

*"The eruption came on gradually at first, getting larger and larger until finally it broke out in a roar like thunder. The smoke cloud was hurled with tremendous velocity many miles high, and the rocks thrown from the crater were seen to fly way below the timberline."*

**B. F. LOOMIS**

CHAPTER TWO

# PRESERVING

**GRAND TETON NATIONAL PARK | WYOMING**

The Snake River flows free beneath the Teton Range. Amid great controversy, the valley and its centerpiece river gained park status in 1950.

# the WONDERS

# Preserving the Wonders
## 1917–1933

—◦◦◦—

*"Horace, what God-given opportunity has come our way to preserve wonders like these before us? We must never forget or abandon our gift."*

### STEPHEN T. MATHER

*first director of the National Park Service,
to his assistant Horace Albright*

Stephen T. Mather, the man who would become the first director of the National Park Service, walked into his destiny almost by happenstance, and on a dare. After five years as a reporter with the *New York Sun,* he turned to business and made a fortune in the borax industry. Still, he felt restless, unfulfilled. The mountains were calling. While hiking in the High Sierra in 1914, he found the areas around Yosemite and Sequoia National Parks so despoiled by timbermen, cattle, and sheep, and the parks themselves crippled by

**MOUNT RUSHMORE NATIONAL MEMORIAL SOUTH DAKOTA**

During the 1930s, the face of Abraham Lincoln takes shape on Mount Rushmore. Nearly 400 people worked on the sculptures of Abraham Lincoln, George Washington, Thomas Jefferson, and Theodore Roosevelt; the work was dangerous, but no lives were lost.

See America First
GREAT NORTHERN RAILWAY "See America First" Glacier National Park

THE GREAT NORTHWEST
Annotated Time Table

poor management, that he wrote a complaint to Secretary of the Interior Franklin K. Lane, who, like Mather, had attended the University of California. The two men met later in Chicago, where Lane invited Mather to run the new agency himself. Would he take the bait? John Muir was gone. Others had to carry the banner. Lane knew Mather as a keen outdoorsman and a member of the Sierra Club and as a born leader with all the attributes the national parks needed: passion, vision, excellent connections, money, and a gift for public relations. Lane invited Mather to Washington and there introduced him to a bright young law student who worked at the Department of the Interior, Horace M. Albright. The torch was lit.

⸺⬦⸺

OVER THE NEXT DECADE and a half (1917-1933), these two men, so alike yet so different from each other, initiated a golden flowering of the NPS that continued for more than half a century. They were in the right place at the right time, and they knew it, as they expanded the family of national parks from south to north and west to east, and from scenery into history. Among their accomplishments were Mount McKinley, Grand Canyon, Acadia, Carlsbad Caverns, Bryce Canyon, Mammoth Cave, Grand Teton, Badlands, Isle Royal, White Sands, and Death Valley National Parks; plus the White House, the Statue of Liberty, the Lincoln Memorial, and others; and, transferred from the War Department, the most hallowed Civil War grounds in American history: Antietam, Shiloh, Gettysburg, Vicksburg, and Appomattox Courthouse, to name a few.

⸺⬦⸺

"MATHER REENERGIZED THE CAMPAIGN for a new bureau, courting prominent writers, publishers, businessmen, and politicians," NPS historian Richard West Sellars wrote. "[He] and Horace Albright worked steadily with their key congressional contacts . . . Mather also gained widespread attention for the national parks, encouraging two highly popular magazines, the *Saturday Evening Post* and the *National Geographic,* to give the parks special coverage. The latter publication devoted its April 1916 issue to the 'See America First' theme."

. . . . . . . . . . . . . . . . . . . . . . . . . . . . . .

According to National Park
Service designer Keith
Hoofnagle, legendary
Superintendent Frank
Pinkley (far left, with his
staff) "revealed an uncanny
ability to explain, instruct,
and cajole in a fatherly way."

*BELOW:*
**LUGGAGE LABEL
GLACIER NATIONAL PARK**

. . . . . . . . . . . . . . . . . . . . . . . . . . . . . .

"Playground of the Northwest"
was how the Great Northern
Railway promoted Glacier
National Park. The park's
primary developer, Great
Northern sold such items
as this 1910 mountain goat
luggage tag.

It worked. After much puffing and blowing on Capitol Hill, the National
Park Service was established on August 25, 1916. The enabling legislation, the
so-called Organic Act, specified that the parks be both used and preserved.
Mather regarded it as a double mandate: not easy to achieve, but not impossible
either. Earlier that month, Lassen Volcanic and Hawaii Volcanoes National
Parks had been created. Now Mather and Albright could turn their attention
north, from lands of lava and fire to a subarctic world of ice and snow, a land
rich with bears, caribou, moose, and wolves, and the world's only species of
wild white sheep.

———

ALASKA'S MOUNT MCKINLEY NATIONAL PARK, established in February 1917, was the first national park founded after the birth of the
National Park Service, and the first designed to protect wildlife
above scenery. (The park was tripled in size and renamed Denali
National Park in 1980.) It all began with Charles Sheldon, a wealthy
naturalist and Yale University graduate cut from the same conservation cloth as Teddy Roosevelt. Like T. R., Sheldon loved to hunt but
detested slaughter. After spending many months in the Denali region
from 1906 to 1908, finding it inspiring and restful even in winter's bitter

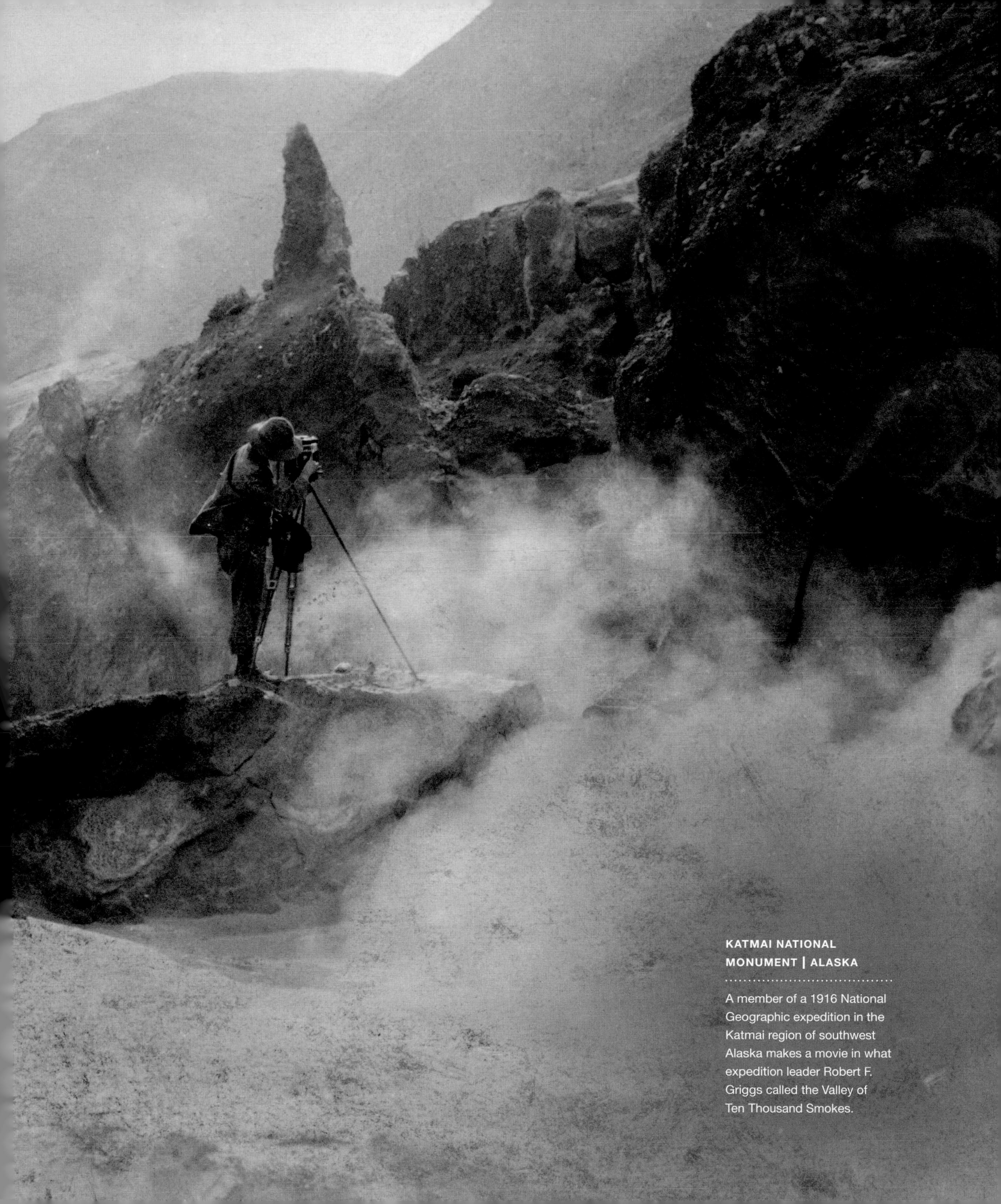

**KATMAI NATIONAL MONUMENT | ALASKA**

A member of a 1916 National Geographic expedition in the Katmai region of southwest Alaska makes a movie in what expedition leader Robert F. Griggs called the Valley of Ten Thousand Smokes.

cold, he witnessed how easily Dall sheep could be shot to extinction. He'd gunned down seven rams himself, in less than one minute, and packed the skulls and horns for museums back East. If Sheldon, who considered himself an "indifferent marksman," could so easily decimate one band of rams, imagine the slaughter that commercial market hunters could inflict as they combed the foothills of the Alaska Range, eager to supply wild meat to railroad workers and gold prospectors flooding into the country.

# STEPHEN MATHER

The first director of the National Park Service (1916-1929), Stephen T. Mather worked tirelessly to promote the parks. He arm-twisted railroad tycoons, congressmen, and journalists, at times spending his own money to pay salaries and procure valuable tracts of land. He created the image of the park ranger as a person of virtue and also helped design roads that fit gracefully into wild landscapes. While he supported predator control, he also masterminded the first conference on state parks to help build a preservation land ethic at local levels. In 1930, as he lay dying, his final words expressed hope for more parks. Bronze plaques cast in Mather's honor today read, "There will never come an end to the good he has done." ■

While Sheldon worked his contacts in the influential Boone and Crockett Club, another park advocate, artist and mountaineer Belmore Browne, worked his allies in the Camp Fire Club. Each trod gently. Powerful men opposed them, especially Judge James Wickersham, delegate of the territory of Alaska, who sympathized with gold prospectors in the Kantishna Hills, near Wonder Lake, immediately north of Mount McKinley, where Wickersham himself had staked claims. In time, however, the park idea gained support. Mather and Albright came on board, as did William T. Hornaday, director of the New York Zoological Society. Browne testified before Congress, "Giant moose still stalk the timberline valleys; herds of caribou move easily across the moss-covered hills; bands of white big-horn sheep look down on the traveler from frowning mountains, while at any time the powerful form of the grizzly bear may give the crowning touch to the wilderness picture. But while the Mount McKinley region is the fountainhead from which come the herds of game that supply the huge expanse of south-central Alaska, that fountainhead is menaced. Slowly but surely the white man's civilization is closing in, and already sled loads of dead animals from the McKinley region have reached the Fairbanks market. Unless a refuge is set aside, in which the animals that remain can breed and rear their young unmolested they will soon follow the buffalo." They'll vanish. Browne added, "The great good that has come with our national expansion has always been followed by evils. Are we a nation able to profit by our mistakes? Can these tragedies be prevented? Yes: but our last and only chance lies in the Mount McKinley region."

SCIENTISTS | KATMAI
NATION AL MONUMENT

..................................

Chemists collect gas from a
fumarole in Katmai National
Park, where more than a
dozen active volcanoes
exist. Research began when
scientists discovered the
Valley of Ten Thousand
Smokes only four years
after the cataclysmic 1912
Novarupta-Katmai eruption.
Katmai became a national
monument in 1918, a national
park in 1980.

WHILE THE BILL TO ESTABLISH Mount McKinley National Park worked its
way through Congress, two other men, both scientists and members of the
Ecological Society of America, strove to protect other parts of Alaska. Bot-
anist Robert F. Griggs led a 1916 National Geographic expedition into the
Katmai Region and discovered what he called the "Valley of Ten Thousand
Smokes," a surreal, ash-filled area, once verdant green, now patterned with
countless fumaroles in the aftermath of a mighty volcanic eruption. And
William S. Cooper, also a botanist and a kind and quiet man who had read
John Muir, journeyed into Glacier Bay to establish vegetation plots he would
visit over the next 50 years to better understand the process of primary plant
succession: how life reclaims a deglaciated landscape that's been scoured
down to bedrock.

In early 1917, Congress passed the bill creating Mount McKinley National
Park. One week later, Charles Sheldon hand delivered it to President Woodrow Wilson for his signature. The next year, Katmai National Monument was
established by executive order. And in 1925, President Calvin Coolidge made
the same commitment to Cooper's dream when he established Glacier Bay
National Monument.

SOMETHING WAS AFOOT. The same momentous summer that Robert Griggs explored Katmai, and William Cooper Glacier Bay, the National Park Service began to define itself and a new American century. Stephen Mather and Horace Albright visited Jackson Hole, a stunning valley south of Yellowstone, set perfectly beneath the Tetons, and decided it had to be a national park: from mountaintop to valley. But how? Already much of the valley land was in private hands. And the people of Wyoming were not to be trifled with.

In the final year of his presidency, Teddy Roosevelt had established the 800,000-acre Grand Canyon National Monument, an area larger than Rhode Island. Many Arizonans never forgave him. Politicians threatened lawsuits. T. R. didn't care. "Surely," he said, "our people do not understand even yet the rich heritage that is theirs."

But they would one day. In February 1919, six weeks after Roosevelt died, Mather and his team finally succeeded in getting the Grand Canyon preserved as a national park— no easy task when opposed by hustlers and scoundrels who passed themselves off as patriots. Equally as significant, on that same February day, Maine's Sieur de Monts National Monument was renamed Lafayette National Park, becoming the first national park in the eastern United States, and the first created by donations of private land; ten years later the name was changed to Acadia, a French term meaning "heaven on earth."

Next came Carlsbad Caverns and Bryce Canyon National Parks, in 1923 and 1924, respectively, together with many more national monuments, most of them in the desert southwest. From there Mather continued to push east, wanting national parks in the Appalachians, which he called "the greatest outstanding peaks east of the Rocky Mountains." If most Americans couldn't travel to their national parks out in Arizona, California, and Oregon, 2,000 and 3,000 miles away, Mather said he'd bring the parks to them. He made a plan: Establish national parks within one or two days' travel from Boston and Washington, D.C. (to make an impression on members of Congress), and from Philadelphia, Roanoke, and Atlanta. Make parks accessible, relevant, part of the American experience, and places to drive *to* and *through*. Build roads, museums, and other welcoming facilities. Have visitors be greeted by a park ranger who's always kind, competent, and knowledgeable. Make states proud to have their own national park.

Over a long weekend in 1918, Albright had written a "creed" for the National Park Service, which said, among many things, that the parks must be "maintained in absolutely unimpaired form." He delivered it to Secretary Lane to

**CARLSBAD CAVERNS NATIONAL PARK NEW MEXICO**

................................................

Formed when sulfuric acid dissolved the surrounding limestone of the Guadalupe Mountains, Carlsbad Caverns consists of 119 known caves below a desert landscape of ancient seabed escarpments and deep canyons.

*OPPOSITE:*

**WHALE BOX | GLACIER BAY NATIONAL MONUMENT**

................................................

A bent-wood box with a killer whale design epitomizes the artwork—both practical and beautiful—of the Tlingit Indians who hunted and fished in the Glacier Bay region for countless generations.

appear as a letter from Lane to Mather (thereby giving the letter more political weight). "There are four general functions fulfilled by the national parks," Albright later told a women's club: "the development of physical health and the desire for outdoor life on the part of the citizens; the development of a broader mental horizon and the education of the people in the ways and habits of wild animals, birds, and natural history; the development of a national patriotism; the diversion of the tourist travel from foreign countries and the retaining of the money spent by American tourists abroad in this country."

Were Mather and Albright too late to save vast stands of the mixed hardwood-softwood forests that gave the Appalachians their stunning color and texture? Forests within an hour's drive of tens of millions of Americans? One report said much of the Appalachians had been so severely logged as to appear "skinned." To Mather's relief, the Southern Appalachian National Park Committee, established by Secretary of the Interior Hubert Work, reported on

........................................

*"He is a better citizen with a keener appreciation of the privilege of living here who has toured the national parks."*

## STEPHEN T. MATHER

........................................

"several areas . . . that contained topographic features of great scenic value," places that remained pristine only by "their inaccessibility and the difficulty of profitably exploiting the timber wealth that mantles the steep mountain slopes." Soon though, those forests would be at risk of being cut.

Mather, Albright, and their allies moved with careful deliberation. The land was private, mostly farms; every acre would need to be purchased. Despite some resistance, a wave of excitement swept through the region. "Swayed by this outburst of citizen support," historian Alfred Runte wrote, "in May 1926 Congress authorized the secretary of interior to accept, on behalf of the federal government, a maximum of 521,000 acres and 704,000 acres for Shenandoah and Great Smoky Mountains national parks respectively." The estimated cost: two and half million dollars for Shenandoah; ten million dollars for Great Smoky Mountains. Staggering sums back then. Still, thousands of citizens from Virginia, Tennessee, and North Carolina—many of them dirt poor—heard

# SPOTLIGHT ON THE CIVIL WAR

# U.S.S. *CAIRO* ARTIFACTS

To win the American Civil War, Union forces had to weaken the Confederacy by taking control of the lower Mississippi River. The town of Vicksburg was key, and heavily fortified. On a cold December morning in 1862, the ironclad gunboat U.S.S. *Cairo* led a small flotilla up the Yazoo River, near Vicksburg, to destroy Confederate batteries and clear the channel of underwater mines (torpedoes). Suddenly the flotilla came under fire. The *Cairo* made guns ready and turned toward shore when two massive explosions ripped gaping holes in its hull. It sank in 12 minutes in 36 feet of water, with no loss of life. Over the decades the *Cairo* became entombed in silt, lost in forgotten memories. Not until the 1950s did Edwin Bearss, historian at Vicksburg National Military Park, discover the vessel. Its artifacts revealed what the National Park Service calls "a treasure trove of weapons, munitions, naval stores and personal gear of the sailors who served on board." ■

①

②

③

④

⑤

**U.S.S. *CAIRO* ARTIFACTS**
**VICKSBURG NATIONAL**
**MILITARY PARK,**
**MISSISSIPPI**
......................................
1. Flask; 2. Wooden chest;
3. Copper tea kettle; 4. Shaving brush; 5. Fifes.

~ 118 ~

**U.S.S. *CAIRO* ARTIFACTS
VICKSBURG NATIONAL
MILITARY PARK,
MISSISSIPPI**

........................................

6. Medicine bottles;
7. Clysters (syringes) and
ointment box; 8. Wrist irons
(for disciplining crew
members); 9. Pipes; 10.
Navy-issue leather shoes.

about the campaign through word of mouth, in churches and along roads, in newspapers, or from local politicians, and they pitched in. Students donated every cent raised in their high school plays. Kids raided their piggy banks. Hiking groups and botany clubs made donations and appealed to local pride: If the West could have its great national parks, so could the East. The logging industry fought back with full-page newspaper ads, but the donations poured in unabated. The people of Appalachia wanted their own national parks and were willing to pay for their states to purchase the land (that would then be donated to the federal government to make the parks). When each fund drive fell short by half the required amount, all seemed lost until a mysterious benefactor came to the rescue. At first he kept a low profile; he had another national park to work on, this one out West.

———

WITH A SHORT-CROPPED BEARD and a bandanna tied loosely around his neck, the man known as Mr. Davison raised no suspicions with his land-purchase inquiries among the ranchers and farmers of Jackson Hole, the 60-mile-long valley that ran north-south below the Tetons. He was in fact John D. Rockefeller, Jr., the only son of John D. Rockefeller, Sr., America's first billionaire and the founder of the Standard Oil Company, which controlled more than 90 percent of the oil sold in the United States. Two years earlier, John Jr. had donated $50,000 to help clean up the roads of Yellowstone. And before that, he'd helped seal the deal that became Lafayette National Park. All because his wife, Abby, a New Englander, so loved the wild Maine coast. Now, in the summer of 1926, as he and Abby visited Jackson Hole, he asked his driver, Horace Albright, then superintendent of Yellowstone, about ranchers and their grazing rights, and farmers who wanted to build dams for irrigation, and why the U.S. Forest Service always seemed to oppose the new National Park Service. A lover of sunsets and trees since boyhood, Rockefeller asked why that old building stood where it did, blocking the view? And why telephone lines were on the west side of the road, where they also diminished the view. Abby criticized unsightly billboards and a burned-out gas station. Albright said little. He had to choose his words—and timing—wisely.

As far back as 1882, Civil War hero Gen. Philip Sheridan had noted that Yellowstone National Park should be extended south into Jackson Hole to protect the nation's largest remaining elk herd. Now, 40-some years later, with the valley mostly settled and fenced by people with a strong sense of entitlement, that idea was anathema. Albright stopped the car near the end of the day and shared his dream of a national park, one that contained not just the mountains but the valley as well, a good portion of it anyway. The Rockefellers listened. "When I finished," Albright wrote, "they remained silent as we watched the sun disappear behind the jagged peaks, casting long, sharp shadows across the valley . . . I felt a little let down." The Rockefellers made no comment.

Four months later, Albright received an invitation to visit Rockefeller in New York City. When again he told the philanthropist about a few select lands that could possibly be purchased at the base of the mountains, around Jackson Lake, Rockefeller interrupted, "I remember you used the word 'dream.'" Correct, Albright said. Rockefeller announced that his family wasn't interested in pieces; they wanted the entire valley, what he called "an ideal project"—a dream project. Albright couldn't believe it. A national park that might one

**PEOPLE IN THE PARKS**

# HORACE ALBRIGHT

Dressed in a borrowed suit and living at the local YMCA, Horace M. Albright was a poor 24-year-old law student working for Secretary of the Interior Franklin Lane when he became Stephen Mather's assistant at the newly created National Park Service. "He's old enough to be my father," Albright said of his new boss. Over the years, they formed a great partnership: Mather with his skills in public relations, and Albright with his connections in Washington, D.C. Young Horace learned fast and orchestrated many of his own triumphs while serving as second director of the NPS from 1929 to 1933. Like Mather, he'd grown up in California and had the good fortune to meet John Muir, an encounter that changed his life. ■

day encompass the mountains and valley as one? He drew up a plan: 30,000 acres to be purchased from nearly 400 willing landowners for a total cost of over one million dollars. When Grand Teton National Park was established in 1929, it encompassed the mountains and a few lakes, but none of the valley. Rockefeller continued his quiet purchases. A year later the plot was exposed. All across Wyoming, the philanthropist was labeled as a feudal lord and other things not so polite. The fight to preserve Jackson Hole had not ended. It was just beginning. Over the decades, it became the most contentious battle in the history of the National Park Service.

———❦———

**SNARE DRUM | GUILFORD COURTHOUSE NATIONAL MILITARY PARK**

...................................

A snare drum survived the American Revolutionary War battle of Guilford Courthouse, North Carolina, in March 1781, when British commander Lt. Gen. Lord Cornwallis said the Americans, under the command of Gen. Nathanael Greene, "fought like demons."

**STATUE OF LIBERTY NATIONAL MONUMENT NEW YORK**

...................................

A worldwide symbol of freedom and open immigration, the Statue of Liberty, dedicated in 1886, stands on Liberty Island, at the mouth of the Hudson River. This image, the first successful aerial photograph, used the Finlay process, one of the first methods of making color photographs.

IN 1933, IN HIS FIRST 105 DAYS, Franklin Delano Roosevelt and his administration moved 15 major bills through Congress in what historian Arthur Schlesinger, Jr., called a "presidential barrage of ideas and programs unlike anything known to American history." They included the Agricultural Adjustment Act, the Glass-Steagall Act, and the Civilian Conservation Corps.

In the midst of this, Roosevelt invited Horace Albright on a day trip to inspect a fishing lodge in the Shenandoah Valley. Stephen Mather had retired in 1929 and died one year later. As the new director of the NPS, Albright sought to expand its authority over America's rich heritage—natural and cultural. Albright found a sympathetic ear in Roosevelt. According to NPS historian

John Sprinkle, "FDR and [Secretary of the Interior Harold] Ickes saw the need for engendering a renewed appreciation for American history . . . during the depths of the Great Depression when the fundamental institutions of the American experiment had failed so miserably." Added NPS historian Robert Sutton, "When they returned to Washington, FDR asked Albright to put his money where his mouth was and to prepare a proposal along the lines of what he had suggested." Albright did, and within days, on June 10, 1933, Roosevelt signed two executive orders for a federal government reorganization that transferred from the War Department and Agriculture Department (U.S. Forest Service) 64 national monuments, battlefield sites, and national capital parks—all to the National Park Service. Critics cried foul from both ends of the ideological spectrum. Robert Sterling Yard, Mather's former publicist, feared that the National Park Service (and the great national parks themselves) would be ruined by "the fatal belief that different standards can be maintained in the same system without the destruction of all standards." Gifford Pinchot, chief nemesis of John Muir during the Hetch Hetchy debate, sought to subsume the Park Service into his darling: the U.S. Forest Service. Thanks to FDR, that threat disappeared. "The order of June 10," Albright summarized, "effectively made the Park Service a very strong agency."

Having opened its arms to the responsibility of preserving American history, the Service faced many challenges. Some new, some old. Among them: the practice of predator control in the face of the new sciences of ecology and wildlife biology. ■

**GETTYSBURG NATIONAL MILITARY PARK PENNSYLVANIA**

..............................

From Little Round Top, visitors survey where everything changed during the American Civil War. In July 1863, Gen. Robert E. Lee's invading Confederate Army was turned back south on a journey that would end with Lee's surrender to Gen. Ulysses S. Grant in April 1865.

# BOLD GROWTH

## 1917–1933

THE U.S. NATIONAL PARK SERVICE grew and matured quickly in its first 15 years, all under the leadership of two remarkable men, Stephen T. Mather and Horace M. Albright, who enjoyed something of a father-son relationship. Their objective was simple: create as many parks as possible. As the world become more crowded and industrial—and waged war on nature itself—people turned to their parks with a greater need for rest, education, and inspiration.

**BADLANDS NATIONAL PARK | SOUTH DAKOTA**

A summer storm brews over the Badlands' eroded buttes and spires and mixed-grass prairie, where four species of mammals have been reintroduced to their native habitat: the black-footed ferret, bighorn sheep, bison, and swift fox.

## FROM THE ARCHIVES

# DENALI

"BELT FASTENED TIGHT?" shouted Dr. Terry Moore above the sputtering of the airplane's idling engine. I nodded. "Okay, here we go!" Our little two-seated single-engine craft started bumping down the gravel runway of the airport at Chelatna Lake, 100 miles northwest of Anchorage, Alaska.

In another moment we were off on an adventure which already had my heart pounding with mixed feelings of excitement and, I must admit, a certain amount of apprehension.

Ahead of us, though invisible in a blanket of fog, towered the 20,300-foot snow-capped cone of mighty Mount McKinley, loftiest peak in North America.

McKinley was named in 1896 for Republican presidential nominee of that year by W. A. Dickey, who was prospecting in the vicinity. Long before, the Alaskan natives had called it, more appropriately, Denali, the Great One. It had been climbed only six times before our 1951 assault.

We were going to try what time after time had been declared impossible—to climb McKinley's rugged West Buttress. More exciting still, we were going to try to do at least a third of the climb by airplane.

To accomplish this, Terry Moore would have to land his tiny plane on the unexplored surface of Kahiltna Glacier.

Bradford Washburn, "Mount McKinley Conquered by New Route," *National Geographic,* August 1953

**DENALI NATIONAL PARK | ALASKA**

Seventeen major glaciers (and many smaller ones) spill off the central Alaska Range that runs through the mountainous heart of Denali National Park. Crowning the park is Mount McKinley, the highest point in North America (at 20,320 feet); it's also known as Denali, an Athabascan Indian word meaning "the high one."

"To the brown bear
almost everything is food except granite."
**JOHN MUIR**

**KATMAI NATIONAL PARK | ALASKA**

A coastal brown bear *(Ursus arctos)* fishes for sockeye salmon at Brooks Falls, fattening up for a long winter sleep, when it will go months without eating. As cubs, bears often learn fishing techniques from their mothers.

## FROM THE ARCHIVES

# THE GRANDEST CANYON

I RETREATED FROM THE CROWDED hotel lobby to the overlook from which I had first seen the canyon. I've seen it often since. The magic never fades. But like a first love the first visit can never be repeated—and nothing can prepare you for it.

Forested slopes leading to the rims give no warning. As you walk the last few feet, the world suddenly slides away, leaving you hovering uncertainly over a forbidding abyss. It's as if nature has carved a monument to itself—a majestic phenomenon that hushes all but the most insensitive.

Gravity pulls at your soul. Your mind reaches for something familiar. Distance, depth, and time seem infinite. You sense more than see an opposite rim far away.

In gaudy rock layers the skeleton of the earth lies exposed. Without being told, you know that down there lie answers to questions about the birth of the earth.

Light and shadows flow among towering buttes in perpetual slow motion with no two moments alike—ever. When the weather's at its worst, the drama's at its best. Afternoon storms fester around sun-warmed buttes and rumble from valley to valley. Lightning stabs at the peaks —sometimes in crisp white thrusts, sometimes as flickers behind curtains of mist.

The spectacle frightens some people.

W. E. Garrett, "Grand Canyon: Are We Loving It to Death?" *National Geographic,* July 1978

**GRAND CANYON NATIONAL PARK | ARIZONA**

Most visitors to the Grand Canyon drive to the south rim and spend less than an hour there admiring the vistas and taking photos. A few hike the trails, descending through the eons measured by the layer-cake strata, one rocky formation beneath another, deeper and deeper into the canyon, going back tens and hundreds of millions of years. And still others—such as these fun-lovers on the Little Colorado River—play in the heart of it all.

**HOVENWEEP NATIONAL MONUMENT | UTAH-COLORADO**

On today's Utah-Colorado border, storm light catches Castle Ruin, a Puebloan-era structure (A.D. 900-1200) whose exact function still mystifies archaeologists. Hunter-gatherers lived in this area for thousands of years before the Puebloans arrived and distinguished themselves by farming; they probably left because of drought or conflict with neighboring Indians, or both.

*OPPOSITE:*

**HOT SPRINGS NATIONAL PARK | ARKANSAS**

Known as the "American Spa," the ancient and soothing thermal waters of Hot Springs, Arkansas, began attracting visitors in the early 1800s. From the 1880s until the 1940s, its waters hosted several major league baseball teams (the Chicago White Stockings, Cincinnati Reds, Pittsburgh Pirates, and Boston Red Sox), whose players soaked away their aches and pains in state-of-the-art facilities, including ornately tiled tubs.

**CARLSBAD CAVERNS NATIONAL PARK | NEW MEXICO**

Artificial lighting gives color, dimension, and depth to the limestone formations of Carlsbad Caverns. Jim White first explored these caverns in the late 1890s and named many of the passageways and larger rooms, but he had trouble convincing his neighbors that the caves existed.

## FROM THE ARCHIVES

# BRYCE CANYON

AS WE EXPLORED the stony fairyland of Bryce, I recalled surveyor T. C. Bailey, who came on the scene 80 years ago and decided it was the wildest and most wonderful sight the eye of man had ever beheld. "There are thousands of red, white, purple, and vermilion rocks, of all sizes," he reported, "resembling sentinels on the walls of castles, monks and priests in their robes, attendants, cathedrals and congregations."

Today many of the most distinctive rocks, ranging from the size of a man to hundreds of feet high, have names of their own: the Turtle, the Gossips, the Happy Family, Thor's Hammer, the Organ Grinder's Monkey, and dozens more. But Buzz couldn't resist the name-it-yourself urge. He thought the pillars known as the Three Wise Men looked like a battery of guided missiles, "all set to blast off."

As for me, at first I couldn't see the rock named Queen Victoria as anything but that illustrious monarch. And then I got a view from an unusual angle, and the Queen changed into a bear on its hind legs.

Soon we discovered that as light and shadow varied with the time of day, so did the shapes of rocks and the amazing array of colors.

William Belknap, Jr., "Nature Carves Fantasies in Bryce Canyon," *National Geographic,* October 1958

**BRYCE CANYON NATIONAL PARK | UTAH**

It was "a helluva place to lose a cow," said pioneer Ebenezer Bryce, sent by the Mormon Church in the 1870s to settle a picturesque area in southwest Utah. Ebenezer and his wife, Mary, lived directly below the beautiful amphitheater of hoodoos (fingerlike pinnacles of soft limestone) and other geographic features that today bear their name.

**GLACIER BAY NATIONAL PARK | ALASKA**

"And now I understand . . . all the old attempts at description," wrote author-photographer Dave Bohn upon seeing the tidewater glaciers of Glacier Bay. "I understand why they were written and why they failed."

**GLACIER BAY NATIONAL PARK | ALASKA**

.......................................

Two hundred and fifty years ago Glacier Bay was all glacier and no bay. Today, it's 70 miles long and up to 10 miles wide: a land and sea of resilience, a living scientific laboratory, and an ancient Tlingit homeland coming back to life (with orcas, above, and Nootka lupine wildflowers, opposite), all in the wake of the fastest recorded glacial retreat in history.

FROM THE ARCHIVES

# GLACIER BAY

SINCE VANCOUVER'S TIME that mass has retreated 59 miles and split into a dozen smaller tributary glaciers, sequestered at the ends of their fjordlike inlets. A new land has been unveiled: Pioneering plants have taken root, new wildlife populations have moved in—bears, moose, wolves, and squirrels on land; whales, seals, porpoises, and fish at sea. They move as always in their own mysterious ways, flexing to laws we barely comprehend, raising their young in the contours of a geography cut and carved by ice.

Time condenses here. Processes normally measured in thousands of years can happen in decades. Some of the glaciers continue to retreat, some are stabilized, others advance. In a single human lifetime you might witness an inlet or a mountain coming out from under the ice or disappearing beneath it. Time isn't on a wristwatch here. It's the river running, the mosses growing, the glaciers flooding and ebbing.

Kim Heacox, "Cruising Alaska Along the Incomparable Inside Passage,"
*National Geographic Traveler,* Summer 1988

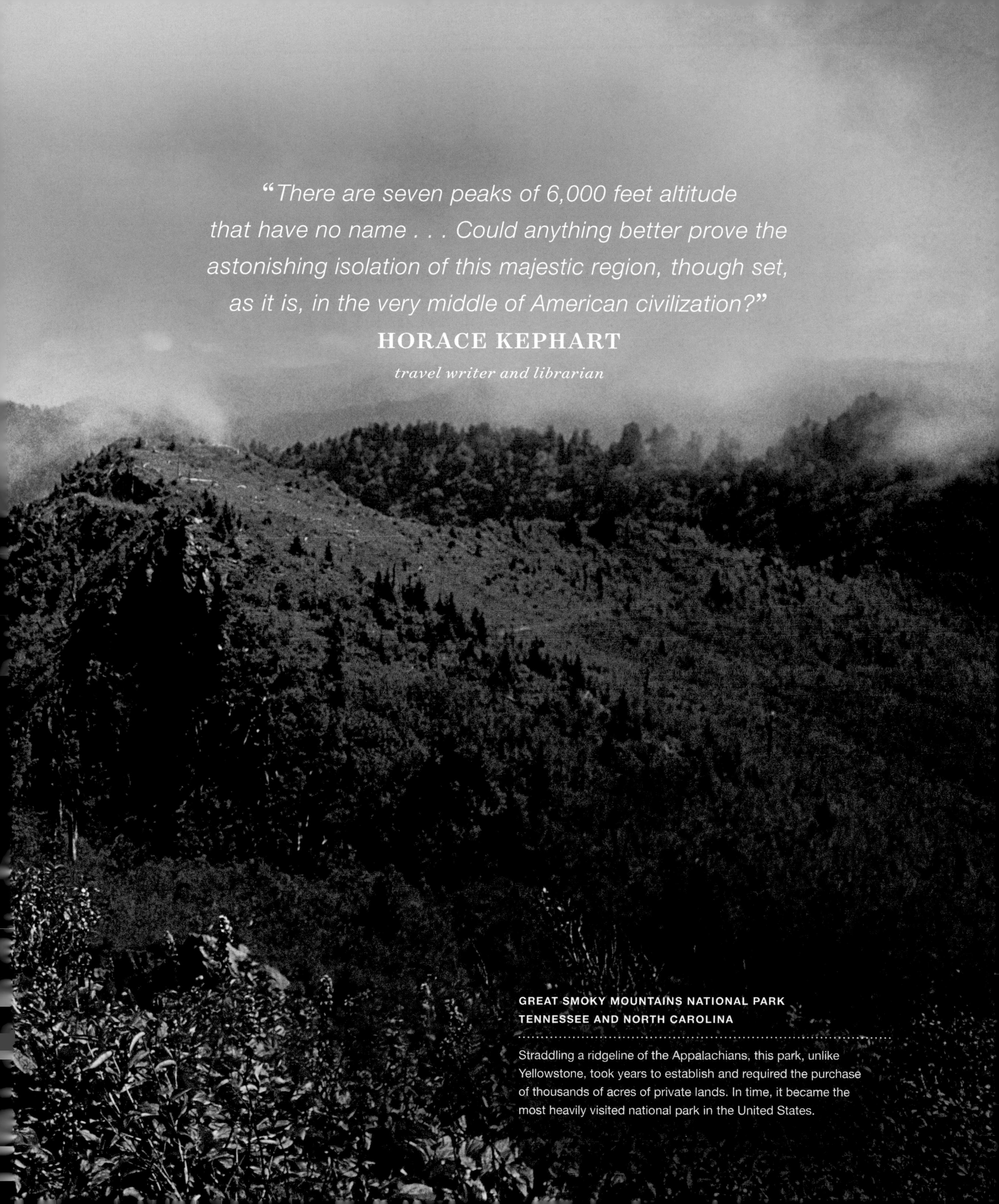

*"There are seven peaks of 6,000 feet altitude
that have no name . . . Could anything better prove the
astonishing isolation of this majestic region, though set,
as it is, in the very middle of American civilization?"*

**HORACE KEPHART**

*travel writer and librarian*

**GREAT SMOKY MOUNTAINS NATIONAL PARK**
**TENNESSEE AND NORTH CAROLINA**

Straddling a ridgeline of the Appalachians, this park, unlike
Yellowstone, took years to establish and required the purchase
of thousands of acres of private lands. In time, it became the
most heavily visited national park in the United States.

## SHENANDOAH NATIONAL PARK | VIRGINIA

At just under 200,000 acres, this park, which runs long and narrow between the Shenandoah River and the Virginia Piedmont, is less than 10 percent of the size of Yellowstone. Yet it has a big reputation as a national treasure. Its close proximity to Washington, D.C. (only 75 miles away), and other urban areas makes it a favorite getaway for millions of annual visitors. While perhaps best known for Skyline Drive, with its many trailheads into the park (to such treats as Dark Hollow Falls, above, and the summit of Bearfence Mountain, right), 40 percent of the park is designated as wilderness.

"*Nowhere else do people from all the states mingle in quite the same spirit as they do in their national parks.*"
**ROBERT STERLING YARD**

**GRAND TETON NATIONAL PARK | WYOMING**

A historic barn stands on Mormon Row in Jackson Hole Valley, offering a simple testimony as the sun descends behind the Teton Range. For many decades, ideologies clashed here. Should man be a gardener—or a guardian—of nature?

## FROM THE ARCHIVES

# ARCHES

IN THE OUTBACK REGIONS of the Colorado Plateau, time stands nearly still. Year by year, erosion lightly planes the mesas and deepens the canyons; a wet year thickens the sparse grasses and a dry year withers them. But the sea of painted rock covering vast stretches of Utah, Arizona, New Mexico, and Colorado remains much as it was before the pioneers, before the Spanish conquistadores, before the first immigrants to the New World.

Shift your timescale from the human to the geologic, though, and the story of these corrugated rockscapes isn't scant change but vast change, hundreds of millions of years of it. Geologists often speak of deep time, the great spans over which the subtlest forces can remake a landscape. The canyonlands are a textbook of deep time.

Mike Edwards, "Rock of Ages,"
*National Geographic,* March 2007

**ARCHES NATIONAL PARK | UTAH**

. . . . . . . . . . . . . . . . . . . . . . . . . . . . . . . . . . . . . . . . . . . . . . . . . . . . . . .

Some 300 million years ago, an inland sea dominated what is today eastern Utah, on the Colorado Plateau. The sea slowly evaporated and the remaining sediment was later blown in by wind to create today's Navajo and Entrada Sandstones. All this weight caused the salt bed below to liquefy and thrust upward into domes. Over millions of years, water froze and expanded in the remaining sandstone cracks and slowly sculpted the rock (mostly Entrada Sandstone) into fantastic arches, spires, and fins, such as Double Arch (left, photographed at night using artificial lighting).

# CANYON DE CHELLY: THEN & NOW

SPECTACULAR WALLS OF RED SANDSTONE rise hundreds of feet above valley floors in Canyon de Chelly National Monument, creating scenes of stunning beauty. Ruins of ancient dwellings can be seen along ledges on the cliffs, while elsewhere in the park dozens of modern Navajo families still live and farm, part of a Native American heritage dating back 2,000 years.

In a unique management arrangement, Canyon de Chelly is administered cooperatively by the National Park Service and the Navajo Nation, within whose tribal lands it lies. Because of the proximity of a living culture to geological features, travel within Canyon de Chelly is more limited than in most parks. Two roads wind along canyon rims, offering superb vistas, and one publicly accessible trail leads down to the canyon floor. Otherwise, visits must be accompanied by a ranger or Navajo guide, the latter available through several local firms. Vehicle tours, horseback rides, hikes, and camping trips can all be arranged, ranging from a few hours to several days.

Though named for its main canyon, the park includes another major canyon, Canyon del Muerto, and smaller side canyons. The two major canyons form a V shape with the park visitor center at its point. Exhibits and a film at the center offer background on both the geologic and human history of the park. Many visitors who want to see more than is available along the rim roads choose to take vehicle tours along the canyon floor. For those with time, horseback rides afford a quieter and more leisurely experience.

However you choose to explore, Canyon de Chelly's blend of enduring culture and beauty makes any visit a memorable experience.

Mel White, *Complete National Parks of the United States*

pre-1916

**SPIDER ROCK | CANYON DE CHELLY NATIONAL MONUMENT**

.......................................

Spider Rock rises 800 feet from the floor of Canyon de Chelly. Navajos here say the top of Spider Rock is home to the mythical Spider Woman, who both protects those who are good and punishes those who disobey.

**WHITE SANDS NATIONAL MONUMENT | NEW MEXICO**

The world's largest gypsum dunefield makes for compelling hiking in New Mexico's Tularosa Basin. While in some places the dunes move very little, elsewhere they may migrate as many as 30 feet in a year.

"*That land is a community is the basic concept of ecology, but that land is to be loved and respected is an extension of ethics.*"
**ALDO LEOPOLD**

**DEATH VALLEY NATIONAL PARK | CALIFORNIA**

................................................................

A full moon sets over the Panamint Range (in the distance) and
the colorful Zabriskie Hills (in the foreground) in Death Valley. First
established as a national monument in 1933, Death Valley became
a national park in 1994, when it was enlarged to 3.73 million acres,
becoming the largest U.S. national park outside Alaska. It is also
the hottest, driest, and lowest national park.

*OPPOSITE:*

**BLACK CANYON OF THE GUNNISON
NATIONAL PARK | COLORADO**

................................................................

While only a little more than 30,000 acres, this park embraces
extreme geologic elements. Among them are canyon-bottom
rocks (Precambrian gneiss and schist) up to 1.7 billion years old;
the Gunnison River, which drops 240 feet per mile, and the Black
Canyon itself, so deep, steep, and narrow that it receives very
little direct sunlight.

## FROM THE ARCHIVES

# WHITE HOUSE

PRESIDENT CALVIN COOLIDGE WENT out for a walk one day with a Senator from Missouri. On their return to the white-pillared Executive Mansion, the Senator said facetiously, "I wonder who lives here."

"Nobody," replied Mr. Coolidge. "They just come and go!"

The remark was only half true. For 166 years [as of 1966] now, Presidents and their families have moved in and out of the Government's 18-acre estate in the heart of Washington. Yet whether their stay was short or long, the men, women, and children who made up that very human cavalcade have truly lived here, with laughter or tears, hope and pride such as other citizens feel. Indeed, it is this personal and domestic life, carried on in the fierce glare of national affairs, that gives the White House its fascinating dual character.

No matter how casual the occasion, there is always a kind of mystery and enchantment, in going behind the scenes here, as I have had occasion to do as a reporter and guest during the last four administrations.

Lonnelle Aikman, "The Living White House," *National Geographic,* November 1966

**PRESIDENT'S PARK (WHITE HOUSE) | WASHINGTON, D.C.**

In the early 1900s a dirt road ran up to the White House, where both horse-drawn carriages and automobiles arrived many times a day, sometimes greeted by the president himself. Built by slaves in the 1790s, the Executive Mansion, as it was then called, survived a burning by British soldiers in the War of 1812 (it didn't reopen until 1817) and finally came to be widely known as the White House during Teddy Roosevelt's presidency (1901-1909). Today, it is part of the 82-acre President's Park, which includes surrounding monuments and open spaces such as the Ellipse and Lafayette Park.

# WASHINGTON MONUMENT: THEN & NOW

ca 1929

**TIDAL BASIN AND
WASHINGTON MONUMENT**
WASHINGTON, D.C.

.......................................

Washington, D.C.'s Potomac
Park and cherry trees lend
greater magnitude to its
signature monument, the
555-foot-tall obelisk constructed between 1848
and 1884 to honor George
Washington's military leadership during the American
Revolutionary War. "[It should]
be of such magnitude and
beauty as to be an object
of pride to the American
people," proposed the Washington National Monument
Society in 1835.

THE ELOQUENT NATURE OF these appeals "to the American people" may be seen in the following extracts from that which appeared in 1846:

"The object was to erect a monument at the seat of Government which should by its colossal magnitude and imposing grandeur exhibit to the remotest age the gratitude of a nation of free men to the man whose excellent good sense and virtues had so pre-eminently contributed to their happiness . . . The hope is still indulged that the American people, influenced by the ardent memory of the great founder of their liberties, will not fail to contribute to the erection of a structure that shall be commensurate with their gratitude and veneration and worthy of him in whose honor it is to be reared . . . A design has been adopted and lithographed . . .

"The pilgrim to Mount Vernon . . . is often shocked when he looks upon the humble sepulcher which contains his dust, and laments that no monument has yet reared its lofty head to mark a nation's gratitude . . . Posthumous honors bestowed by a grateful nation on its distinguished citizens serve the further purpose of stimulating those who survive them to similar acts of greatness and virtue."

Charles Warren, "The Washington National Monument Society,"
*National Geographic,* June 1947

**ANTIETAM NATIONAL BATTLEFIELD | MARYLAND**

Gen. Robert E. Lee's bold invasion of Maryland ended at Antietam on September 17, 1862. Here Confederate and Union troops slaughtered one another in a cornfield, and along a road ("Bloody Lane"), and on a bridge over a creek, in what would be the single bloodiest day of the American Civil War (and in American history): 23,000 soldiers killed, wounded, or gone missing (of the nearly 100,000 engaged).

**SHILOH NATIONAL MILITARY PARK | TENNESSEE**

...................................................................

At daybreak on Sunday, April 6, 1862, thousands of Confederate troops under the command of Gen. Albert Sidney Johnston charged out of the woods to assail Gen. Ulysses S. Grant's Union camps near the Shiloh Meeting House. The two-day battle, a Union victory, resulted in by far the largest number of casualties in any battle in the Civil War to that point; it was a shock to both sides and symptomatic of what was to come.

*OPPOSITE:*

**PETERSBURG NATIONAL BATTLEFIELD | VIRGINIA**

...................................................................

During the ten-month 1864-65 Siege of Petersburg—the longest siege in the history of American warfare—Union troops used this mine entrance (restored) to tunnel under Gen. Robert E. Lee's Confederate positions and lay explosives.

## CHIRICAHUA NATIONAL MONUMENT | ARIZONA

The Apaches called it the "Land of Standing-Up Rocks" (left). While the monument is only 12,000 acres, it offers 17 miles of day-use trails, many of which were built by the Civilian Conservation Corps from 1934 to 1940. In 1976 Congress designated 87 percent of the monument as wilderness. The Chiricahuas, part of the Basin and Range Biogeographical Province, are regarded as "sky islands," mountain ranges surrounded by lower desert grasslands. The monument is a biological crossroads that hosts many species of plants and animals, including 300 species of birds, Chihuahua pine, Douglas and white fir, Arizona cypress, and the agave, or century plant (in full bloom, above).

# OLYMPIC NATIONAL PARK

A NAME CAN SAY A LOT ABOUT a place, or nothing at all. Olympic says a lot. It says that this is as good as it gets. Here, astride the pinnacle of excellence, stands the champion. Fitting, then, that mapmakers should borrow the modifier from mythology and stamp it upon this peninsula poking fist-like into the Pacific at the westernmost edge of the 48 contiguous United States. And if the word suits the peninsula, why not recycle it to the peninsula's national park, overlorded as it is by the mountain Olympus, named for the throne room of the Grecian gods?

John G. Mitchell, "Nature's Champion: Olympic National Park,"
*National Geographic,* July 2004

**OLYMPIC NATIONAL PARK | WASHINGTON**

Beyond its glaciated peaks and lush temperate old-growth rain forests, the park's 60 miles of wild coastline include the easily accessible Ruby Beach (pictured here) with its dramatic sea stacks and headlands.

**DEVILS POSTPILE NATIONAL MONUMENT | CALIFORNIA**

Once part of Yosemite National Park, this small but scenic area was orphaned when a nearby discovery of gold changed Yosemite's southeast boundary—and later was threatened by a proposed hydroelectric dam. Devils Postpile is named after its formations of uniformly and deeply jointed basalt colonnade (60-foot-tall columns of extrusive igneous rock, each column averaging two feet in diameter, above), and known for the Middle Fork of the San Joaquin River that drops 101 feet over that same resistant rock (in Rainbow Falls, left).

**GREAT BASIN NATIONAL PARK | NEVADA**

..........................................

A road less traveled makes its way through a forest of aspens and buttercups in this remote mountain park near the Nevada-Utah border. Here, according to the National Park Service, one can find great diversity, such as "5,000-year-old bristlecone pine trees on rocky glacial moraines," desert, and the Lehman Caves, which were first protected as Lehman Caves National Monument in 1922.

## FROM THE ARCHIVES

# SAGUARO

OUTSTANDING FEATURES OF the Arizona desert are the mountains and the plants. Both come in all sizes, shapes, and colors, and together they give southern Arizona a landscape that seems to the traveler to be "out of this world." In all this strange land the strangest sight, and most characteristic, is the giant cactus *(Cereus giganteus)*, known as the saguaro (or sahuaro).

The principal characteristic of a desert is its little rain, but this desert is freakish in its rainfall. When it is dry, it is exceedingly dry. When a summer rainstorm breaks, the whole country is awash.

The plants of arid regions solve the problem of an irregular water supply either by sending their roots deep toward moisture or by developing large masses of tissue in which water accumulates during the wet periods and forms a reserve to be drawn upon in the long dry spells. In the cactus family, of which the saguaro is monarch, the habit of maintaining a reserve of water is most conspicuously developed.

Forrest Shreve, "The Saguaro, Cactus Camel of Arizona," *National Geographic,* December 1945

**SAGUARO NATIONAL PARK | ARIZONA**

Giant saguaro cacti, emblematic of the Sonoran Desert, ride the skyline beyond Tucson. Two separate units of this park, one east of the city (called the Rincon Mountain District) and the other west (the Tucson Mountain District), bookend Tucson and support a wide diversity of plant and animal species, but the giant saguaros command greatest attention. A single saguaro cactus, 20 feet tall, can weigh 2,000 pounds and be 150 years old.

# CHAPTER THREE

# BROADENING

HALEAKALA NATIONAL
PARK | HAWAII
......................................
On the Island of Maui, visitors
travel by horseback through
the volcanic summit of
Haleakala, a dormant volcano
that last erupted around
500 years ago. *Haleakala* in
Hawaiian means "house
of the sun."

# PERSPECTIVES

# Broadening Perspectives
## 1934–1966

—◆◆◆—

*"Without sunshine, fresh air and open space, man diminishes physically, mentally and emotionally. We need more parks. We need them now, before the cities and highways . . . take all the scenic lands."*

### CONRAD L. WIRTH

On a lonely southern New Mexico highway in February 1936, a car blew a tire, crossed the centerline, and struck an oncoming car carrying Roger Toll, superintendent of Yellowstone, and George Melendez Wright, a young wildlife biologist. Both men died. It was a double loss for the National Park Service. Like Stephen Mather, Wright had a keen ability to see into the future and be an instrument for positive change. He also had money. While Mather had championed tourism in the parks, Wright championed science. In 1929 he conceived of—and personally funded—

**EVERGLADES NATIONAL PARK | FLORIDA**

A rare white morph of a great blue heron perches on a mangrove, where all life is delicately balanced between sea and sky and a future heavy with the storms of change. In the early 1900s, the runaway killing of ornately feathered birds such as this provoked the first calls for conservation in South Florida.

a comprehensive survey to determine how park wildlife populations had crashed and could be restored. "Our national heritage is richer than just scenic features," he wrote. "The realization is coming that perhaps our greatest national heritage is nature itself, with all its complexity and its abundance of life."

For decades, park managers—first the U.S. Army, then the Park Service—had catered to tourists by making "favorite" and "friendly" animals easier to see. The managers shot and trapped coyotes, mountains lions, and wolves; penned up bison: and feed hay to elk, antelope, and deer. In Yellowstone, visitors fed roadside bears like pets, and rangers destroyed white pelican eggs, according to historian Dayton Duncan, "because it was feared that grown pelicans deprived anglers of too many fish." This was not primal America, Wright knew. It was a zoo. "Am I a visionary or just crazy?" he wrote to a fellow scientist as he sought to end what was fast becoming wrongheaded park policy. Intrigued by Wright, Park Service director Horace Albright organized a new wildlife division in 1933 and assigned Wright to be its chief.

In the next two years, Great Smoky Mountains, Shenandoah, Everglades, and Big Bend all became national parks, places that today celebrate biodiversity and ecology—cornerstones of Wright's vision—as much (or more) as scenery. After private donations reached a total of five million dollars, the halfway mark needed to purchase land for Great Smoky Mountains, John D. Rockefeller, Jr., stepped in to pay the shortfall. And for Shenandoah, others in the large Rockefeller family came to the rescue. As if to acknowledge the age of the automobile, plans were made to join the two parks by a 470-mile picturesque ridgetop road called the Blue Ridge Parkway that would eventually have 26 tunnels and more than 300 overlooks. Congress formerly announced the parkway and placed it under NPS jurisdiction in 1936.

As the growing family of national parks opened its arms to greater diversification, perspectives broadened within the Park Service. First came the preservation of grand scenery, then wildlife, then an embrace of history and science and the values they engendered. The Everglades of South Florida—flat, wet, and long considered a good-for-nothing swamp—was anything but national park material in the late 1800s. It had no mountains, bears, or flowering alpine meadows; no glaciers, geysers, granite domes, or tall, ancient trees. A few local plant enthusiasts thought it might qualify as a botanical preserve. William T. Hornaday, one of America's greatest champions of wildlife conservation, visited the Everglades in 1875 and said he found "little that was of special interest, and absolutely nothing that was picturesque or beautiful." The Everglades,

**PHOTOGRAPHIC FIRST
DRY TORTUGAS
NATIONAL PARK**

...........................................

The first underwater color photograph, taken in Dry Tortugas National Park by William Longley and *National Geographic* staff photographer Charles Martin in 1926, helped raise awareness about other natural worlds to be discovered and protected.

*BELOW:*
**COONTIE HAIRSTREAK
EVERGLADES
NATIONAL PARK**

...........................................

Once considered extinct in South Florida, the coontie hairstreak butterfly *(Eumaeus atala florida)* survived because good field science determined the butterfly's host plant was being overharvested, and conservation-minded Floridians took strong measures to save it.

he concluded, is "a long ways from being fit to elevate into a national park, to put alongside the magnificent array of scenic wonderlands that the American people have elevated into that glorious class." Historian Alfred Runte wrote, "Hornaday's rejection of an Everglades national park on the basis of its physical shortcomings underscored how fixed the image of parks as a visual experience had become in the American mind."

In 1904, Governor Napoleon Bonaparte Broward—whose campaign posters proclaimed him as "Florida's Favorite Son"—ran on a populist platform to "Drain the Everglades." The dredges worked fast, and were followed by land speculators who sold tracts still underwater; "land by the gallon," critics cried. Soon vast areas of the north Everglades became covered with cattle ranches and cane fields, disrupting the water flow that is the lifeline for the park. By the 1920s, the critics cried louder, and eloquent voices of dissent began to pepper the landscape. The Everglades, like so many other places, needed—and received—its outspoken defenders just in time: first Ernest F. Coe, a Miami activist alarmed at the disappearance of orchids and egrets, and then Marjorie Stoneman Douglas, a newspaper reporter turned author who wrote, "There are no other Everglades in the world . . . their vast glittering openness, wider than the enormous visible round of the horizon, the . . . sweetness of their massive winds, under the dazzling blue heights of space."

Early in her career, Douglas had written about women's rights and race issues. Then Coe suggested that she apply that same sense of justice to the future of the Everglades. Douglas's words were unassailable: If the Everglades died, she said, so would South Florida. When Horace Albright and George Melendez Wright surveyed the Everglades by hot-air balloon, they were stunned by magnificent flocks of birds and became convinced that it had to be a national park. The bill to establish Everglades National Park passed Congress by a narrow margin in 1934, and forbade any new federal expenditure on the park for five years. Still, it was a beginning. Florida got its second NPS unit, Fort Jefferson National Monument, in the Dry Tortugas, one year later, in 1935.

When the Virgin Islands seemed like a promising place to establish as a national park, thanks to their reefs, beaches, and complex history of civilizations, George Wright went to investigate and quickly endorsed the idea. He then toured the newly established Big Bend National Park, where the Rio Grande River cuts magnificent canyons through the Chisos Mountains of southern Texas. Intelligent, visionary, bilingual (Spanish and English), and likable, Wright served with distinction on a two-nation commission to explore the possibility of an international park on the U.S.-Mexican border. By early in 1936, his wildlife division, composed of 27 biologists, was what Joseph Grinnell, director of the Museum of Vertebrate Zoology at the University of California, called "the supreme hope for pure, uncontaminated wildlife conservation" in America.

Then came Wright's untimely death—a severe setback. "By August 1938, while forestry, landscape architecture, planning and other programs flourished within the Park Service," historian Richard West Sellars wrote, "the number of biologists had dwindled to ten." Among them was Wright's brightest acolyte, Adolph Murie, a man small in stature but large in spirit. Like Wright, Murie was unafraid to speak the unpopular truth. An ecologist years before the word entered the American vocabulary, Murie saw nature as John Muir had: as one vast interconnected system, a symphony of sorts, where each part played an essential role. Murie said fire was a natural element in forest regeneration, and therefore fires must be allowed to burn. He criticized the popular practices

PEOPLE IN THE PARKS

# GEORGE MELENDEZ WRIGHT

George Wright grew up in the San Francisco Bay Area, roaming wild hills and learning the English, Spanish, and scientific names of local plants and animals. He distinguished himself as a keen observer and ecological thinker, and as a friendly presence. Though he died young, at age 31, he was a supernova of the NPS, where he personally funded a service-wide wildlife survey, hired talented biologists, and championed science-based decision-making. To understand how nature works and to secure its best values without destroying it is not "useless idealism," Wright said; "it is good hygiene for civilization." ■

of bear feeding and viewing at the Yellowstone garbage dump. After a two-year study of the park's coyotes, he concluded that inadequate winter range, not predation, was responsible for the falling numbers of bison, mule deer, and elk. Coyotes prey primarily on voles, mice, rabbits, and other small mammals, he said. Only rarely do they eat elk calves in the spring. The superintendent bristled. Soon Murie was shipped north to Alaska, where some thought—incorrectly—that he might never be heard from again. His three-year field study of wolves, Dall sheep, and caribou in Mount McKinley National Park concluded that the wolf—what the Alaska Game Commission called the "villain in Alaska's pageant of wildlife"—was in fact essential to the well-being of everything else. Murie said wolves have a "salutary effect" on prey populations by culling out the old, weak, and injured. They should be protected, not persecuted. This was heresy back in the 1940s, when wolves posed threats—real and imaginary—to many people's livelihoods and property. Murie stood by his claim and over the years called for the reintroduction of wolves in Yellowstone, Grand Teton, Crater Lake, Olympic, Mount Rainier, and Rocky Mountain National Parks, and on Isle Royale, where wolves were so few and moose so plentiful that the park looked akin to what he called a "prosperous barnyard."

It is easy and wrong to play God in a national park, Murie said, echoing Thoreau's dictum that a man is rich in proportion to the number of things he can afford to let alone. "The goal," Murie concluded, "is to have the minimum

**WOLF DEN | PREDATOR AND PREY**

..................................................

Wolves feed a recent kill to their pups outside an Alaskan cave. Fictitious images of heartless, vicious predators filled sportsman magazines and Disney films in the 1940s and '50s, creating an uphill battle for ecologists doing their best to reeducate the public on the important role predators play in keeping prey populations—and entire ecosystems—healthy and robust.

EVERGLADES NATIONAL
PARK | FLORIDA

Roseate spoonbills perch in
the crown of a mangrove.
"If I had to choose," said
pioneering aviator Charles
Lindbergh, "I would rather
have birds than airplanes."

**NAUTICAL CLOCK
CAPE HATTERAS
NATIONAL SEASHORE**

...................................

From the National Park
Service Museum Collections,
this wall-mounted key-wound
brass-plated nautical clock
(5.5 inches in diameter) was
typical of those used by the
U.S. Lighthouse Service
at Cape Hatteras (and elsewhere) in North Carolina in
the early 1900s.

*OPPOSITE:*

**CHANNEL ISLANDS
NATIONAL PARK
CALIFORNIA**

...................................

"Take only photographs,
leave only footprints"
became the credo of low-
impact recreation in the
national parks, exemplified
by this hiker descending a
seaside sand dune on San
Miguel Island.

of manipulation in our parks, to allow, where at all possible, the existing ecological factors, to operate naturally. Let us be guardians rather than gardeners."

———◆———

DESPITE A CRIPPLING DEPRESSION that brought most of the nation to its knees, visitation to the national parks increased fivefold from 1930 to 1939. Franklin Delano Roosevelt's Civilian Conservation Corps put three million young men to work in their national parks and forests and in state parks, planting trees, improving campsites and trails, and building ranger cabins and hiking shelters. Altogether there were 118 CCC camps in NPS units across the country. FDR called them his "CCC boys" and visited them in Shenandoah and Glacier National Parks, where they infused him with a sense of youthfulness. "Here, under trained leadership," he said, "we are helping

..............................................................

**"***If we destroy nature blindly,
it is a boomerang which will be our undoing.***"**

**GEORGE MELENDEZ WRIGHT**

..............................................................

these men help themselves and their families and at the same time are making the parks more available and more useful for the average citizen." Not to be outdone by his fifth cousin from a generation before, FDR used his executive power to establish 11 national monuments, some small, others large: Death Valley, Bandelier, White Sands, Chiricahua, Sunset Crater Volcano, Organ Pipe Cactus, and Tuzigoot, to name a few.

The country's first national seashore, established in 1937 at North Carolina's Cape Hatteras, further advanced the importance of ecological values, what some called the "Everglades effect." It also underscored the notion that private domain needed to be balanced with public domain. "When we look up and down the ocean fronts of America," said FDR's Secretary of the Interior Harold Ickes, "we find that everywhere they are passing behind the fences of private ownership. The people can no longer get to the ocean . . . except by permission of those who monopolize the oceanfront . . . I say it is the prerogative and the duty of the Federal and State Governments to step in and acquire, not a swimming beach here and there, but solid blocks of ocean front hundreds of miles in

**SURFERS | CAPE HATTERAS NATIONAL SEASHORE**

................................................

Thus ends another great day of surfing at Cape Hatteras, North Carolina, where surfers carry their boards back through sunlit beach grass, following a well-used route. One good wind will erase every track.

*BELOW:*

**RED ALGAE | POINT REYES NATIONAL SEASHORE**

................................................

Ranging from Southeast Alaska to Baja California, the red algae *Cryptopleura ruprechtiana*, aka grape tongue, is abundant on the rocky shores of Point Reyes, a short distance north of San Francisco.

length. Call this oceanfront a national park, or a national seashore, or a state park or anything you please—I say that the people have a right to a fair share of it." The cape's open horizon and understated barrier islands, salt marshes, and sand dunes were to be kept "as a primitive wilderness" to best protect "the unique flora and fauna." The Park Service would carefully plan for public facilities to improve the visitor experience and work hard to protect habitat and halt beach erosion. Should any beach fall into private hands, the large estate or simple cottage built as an expression of freedom could easily one day become a housing tract, golf course, or commercial area. And within decades the nesting plovers and sea turtles would be gone. To avoid this takes vision, persistence, and balance. Other national seashores followed, including half a dozen in the 1960s: Cape Cod, Point Reyes, Padre Island, Fire Island, Assateague Island, and Cape Lookout.

⸺⬥⬥⬥⸺

ALTHOUGH SOME OF AMERICA'S greatest seashores gained the protection they needed, many of America's rivers did not. The biggest culprits were pollution and dams. The Army Corps of Engineers and Bureau of Reclamation sought to irrigate and electrify the arid West with nine billion dollars' worth of reservoirs and dams, including ten on the Colorado River, some in national parks. The battle over this "Colorado River Storage Project" came to a head at Echo Park, an unlikely corner on the

Utah-Colorado border where the Green and Yampa Rivers converge in Dinosaur National Monument. President Truman supported the dam, as did Secretary of the Interior Oscar L. Chapman, who said it was in "the interest of the greatest public good." It was Hetch Hetchy all over again. Leading the opposition was David Brower of the Sierra Club and Howard Zahniser of the Wilderness Society. Park Service director Newton Drury opposed the dam, as did his successor, Conrad L. Wirth. Bernard DeVoto, one of America's leading authors, noted that visitation to America's national parks was skyrocketing in the early 1950s. "The attendance will keep on increasing as long as they are worth visiting," DeVoto wrote, "but a good many of them will not be worth visiting if engineers are let loose on them. No one will ever drive 2,000 miles to row a boat [on a reservoir] . . . The only reason why anyone would ever go to Dinosaur National Monument is to see what the Bureau of Reclamation proposes to destroy."

Benton MacKaye spoke to Aldo Leopold's new "land ethic" of nature as a community to which we belong, not a commodity we own. He added that Dinosaur was a beautiful "wilderness that is preserved intact . . . for the field of study . . . the balances of Nature, the web of life, the inter-relationships of species, massive problems of ecology—presently it will not be possible to study such matters anywhere else." Dinosaur National Monument was, in effect, an ancient library—

**GLEN CANYON NATIONAL RECREATION AREA | UTAH**

..........................................

Natural arches, chiseled steps, stunning alcoves, ancient petroglyphs, and a touch of mystery greet hikers who explore Davis Gulch. This area was the last known camp of the enigmatic Everett Ruess, a writer and painter who disappeared from here in 1934.

# NEZ PERCE

"My people, some of them, have run away to the hills, and have no blankets, no food," said Chief Joseph as he surrendered to the U.S. Cavalry a short distance from the Canada border in October 1877. He had evaded capture for months, traveling north with his Nez Perce people. "Hear me, my Chiefs. I am tired; my heart is sick and sad. From where the Sun now stands, I will fight no more forever." A world—and way of life—was coming to an end. Covering 38 sites over four states (Idaho, Montana, Oregon, and Washington), the Nez Perce National Historical Park includes traditional lands that highlight Chief Joseph's 1877 route. It also preserves a stunning array of artwork and living history, including opportunities to watch contemporary Nez Perce artists. ■

**NEZ PERCE ARTIFACTS**
**NEZ PERCE NATIONAL**
**HISTORICAL PARK, IDAHO**

1. Beaded pouch; 2. Beaded buckskin gloves; 3. Rawhide container; 4. Beaded bag (1912); 5. Horse necklace or collar (martingale).

**NEZ PERCE ARTIFACTS
NEZ PERCE NATIONAL
HISTORICAL PARK, IDAHO**

6. Two-skinned dress;
7. Pouch used in material
trade; 8. Painted rawhide bag;
9. Headdress containing 32
eagle feathers; 10. Beaded
moccasins.

a university made of water and stone that if left undefiled could teach us about man's place in the universe for hundreds of generations. Of course, this was gibberish to practical-minded engineers and politicians, whose heads were filled with numbers and dollars. The final vote on the Colorado River Storage Project, with an amendment to exclude the Echo Park Dam, seesawed back and forth until the preservationists prevailed and the final bill stated that "no dam or reservoir constructed under the authorization of the [Colorado River Storage Project] shall be within any National Park or Monument." Historian Roderick Nash would call it the wilderness movement's "finest hour to that date."

Hoover Dam and Glen Canyon Dam, built on the Colorado River, and Grand Coulee Dam, built on the Columbia River, are considered formidable engineering feats. The lakes they impounded became national recreation areas—popular among boaters—administered by the Park Service. Glen Canyon, in particular, flooded by Lake Powell, was a great loss among preservationists, who mounted a belated protest to save it. All across America the question arose again and again: What to do with the land? As Kentucky poet Wendell Berry later summarized, "There are no sacred and unsacred places, only sacred and desecrated places."

———

IN THE LATE 1940s and early 1950s, four of seven Park Service regional directors were historians, men with the long view who were deeply committed to the idea that the national parks could make America a better place— and her people better citizens, as Stephen Mather had said 20 years before. Several of the most popular parks— Yellowstone, Yosemite, and Grand Canyon—were approaching the one-million-visitors-per-year milestone. When Congress refused to enlarge Grand Teton National Park in 1943, FDR signed an executive order establishing Jackson Hole National Monument, east of the park. Many local ranchers and businessmen threatened to start a range war. John D. Rockefeller, Jr., was elated. Now his Jackson Hole land purchases could complement the existing park and monument and make something magnificent. By the time he died in 1960, the great philanthropist had given more than $40 million of his private fortune to public lands conservation.

**LAKE POWELL | GLEN CANYON NATIONAL RECREATION AREA**
...........................................
Boaters play on Lake Powell—waters impounded behind Glen Canyon Dam on the Colorado River.

PEOPLE IN THE PARKS

# CONRAD L. WIRTH

It made perfect sense that Conrad L. Wirth, known as "Connie," found a prosperous career in the National Park Service: He was born in one municipal park and reared in another. His father headed the Minneapolis Parks System for 26 years. Trained as a landscape architect, Wirth joined the NPS as an assistant director in 1931. Under FDR, he excelled at applying Civilian Conservation Corps programs to federal, state, and local parks. As director of the NPS (1951-1964), he conceived of a ten-year one-billion-dollar program—Mission 66, his crowning achievement—to "overcome the inroads of neglect," he said, "and to restore to the American people a National Park System adequate to their needs." Wirth died in 1993, at age 93. ■

Soon came the Kennedy White House, Camelot, *To Kill a Mockingbird,* the Freedom Rides, and Dr. Martin Luther King, Jr.'s "Letter From a Birmingham Jail," inspired in part by Thoreau's "Civil Disobedience," the notion that a man has a moral obligation to gently break an unjust law. The civil rights movement could be tracked over the past three decades by new inclusions in the National Park System: George Washington Carver National Monument in 1943, Booker T. Washington National Monument in 1956, and Frederick Douglass National Historic Site in 1962. When King, a young minister, delivered his "I Have a Dream" speech from the Lincoln Memorial in late August 1963, two park rangers flanked him. In the audience with a quarter million other people was George B. Hartzog, soon to be the new director of the National Park Service. He called King's speech an "everlasting moment." The next year, President Johnson signed the Civil Rights Act and the Wilderness Act. And the year after that came another enlightened piece of legislation: the Land and Water Conservation Fund Act of 1965.

Everything was changing, including the pace of change. During the prosperous and less tumultuous postwar 1950s, Hartzog's predecessor, Conrad Wirth, had proposed and initiated a one-billion-dollar program—the greatest single infusion of money into the Park Service—to regenerate and modernize the national parks and develop a system-wide infrastructure to manage the public and to foster education. Called Mission 66, the program took ten years to complete—in

time for the Park Service's 50th anniversary in 1966. Wirth and others could see that national parks were being loved to death—with cars and lines and litter everywhere—while they fell into disrepair, run on what Bernard DeVoto called a "hot-dog stand budget." Mission 66 aimed to change that. Small, rustic nature centers built in the 1930s by the CCC were replaced by more than 100 modern visitor centers. A few critics said some new centers were incompatible with their sensitive surroundings. And when, against the objections of environmentalists, Mission 66 dollars were spent to pave and realign the Tioga Road in Yosemite, photographer Ansel Adams said the symbol of Mission 66 was the bulldozer. Planners countered that new roads were needed to manage crowds and that visitor centers would not function as museums but rather as facilities to introduce and orient large numbers of people to their parks and get them out among the mountains, flowers, and lakes, where the real education and inspiration begins.

As part of Mission 66, the Park Service also acquired 78 new units, including Virgin Islands, Haleakala, and Canyonlands. And in 1966, the final year of the program, two new national lakeshores, the first of their kind, were established: Pictured Rocks and Indiana Dunes. It was a new and prosperous era for the National Park Service, one that would fade as only the past can, and be looked back upon with nostalgia as a time of deep financial backing and political support. Yet another grand expansion awaited, one that would more than double the acreage in the U.S. National Park System and save America's last great wildernesses as fully intact ecosystems. ■

**NEEDLES DISTRICT CANYONLANDS NATIONAL PARK**

A summer storm rolls over red- and white-banded rock pinnacles that ring a meadow in the Needles district of Canyonlands National Park in Utah. Backcountry hiking and camping is exquisite here for those seeking the remote and restful.

# MODERNIZATION

## 1934–1966

AS IF A REFLECTION of the American dream from one golden shore to another, the U.S. National Park System expanded, diversified, and modernized rapidly after the Great Depression and World War II. The interstate freeway system soon had millions driving 70 miles per hour. More than 100 new park visitor centers were constructed. America got its first national seashores. Rachel Carson wrote Silent Spring. Massive dams were built on great rivers, while other proposed dams were opposed and defeated. All in a struggle to answer Woody Guthrie: If this land is our land, what are we to do with it? Harness it? Or let it be?

**POINT REYES NATIONAL SEASHORE | CALIFORNIA**

Another day ends in golden splendor at California's Point Reyes, a short distance north of San Francisco. Although this 71,000-acre national seashore receives more than two million visitors each year, it provides many opportunities for solitude, and many reminders that nature is more than beauty. It's therapy.

## FROM THE ARCHIVES

# EVERGLADES

THE NATION HAS RECENTLY RECEIVED a magnificent "gift," Everglades National Park, which President Truman dedicated on December 6, 1947. Twenty-eighth such public reserve, it is the only subtropical national park in the United States. A new three-cent stamp has been issued to celebrate the event.

Justified at last were the vision, faith, and unrelenting efforts of 81-year-old Ernest F. Coe, Director of the Everglades National Park Association. For 20 years Coe fought, often single-handed, for creation of a national park in south Florida's unique wilderness.

The Everglades National Park Commission also was instrumental in making the park a reality.

Limits of the park eventually are expected to embrace most of Florida Bay, including nesting keys of the striking, but scarce, roseate spoonbill.

Andrew H. Brown, "Haunting Heart of the Everglades," *National Geographic,* February 1948

**EVERGLADES NATIONAL PARK | FLORIDA**

An eastern diamondback rattlesnake rests on a mangrove tree where the land meets the sea in Florida Bay. In saving places such as the Everglades, America began to awaken to the importance of biodiversity: that parks should preserve not just scenery but also native species and entire ecosystems. Some Floridians called the Everglades a "swamp." Best to drain it, they said. They couldn't have been more wrong.

**THOMAS JEFFERSON MEMORIAL | WASHINGTON, D.C.**

Thomas Jefferson, principal author of the Declaration of Independence (when he was only 33), architect of the Lewis and Clark Expedition, and third president of the United States (among other achievements), stands ever watchful above the slowly rising waters of the East Tidal Basin.

*"Educate and inform the whole mass
of the people . . . They are the only sure
reliance for the preservation of our liberty."*
**THOMAS JEFFERSON**

# THE DRY TORTUGAS

STILL UNFAMILIAR TO MANY AMERICANS are these seven low islands of shell and coral sand which bask in the warm Gulf waters some 70 miles west of Key West, Florida. Mention of them frequently elicits a blank stare and the query, "What and where are the Dry Tortugas?"

Yet on one of the islands, Garden Key, sprawls historic old Fort Jefferson, now a National Monument. This fortress which never fired a shot in war has known its share of death and drama. It once served as the Nation's loneliest prison, and here Dr. Samuel A. Mudd, of Maryland, imprisoned for setting the broken leg of Lincoln's assassin, rose from chains to lead the heroic fight against the 1867 yellow fever epidemic which sowed these sands with graves.

Aside from those familiar with Fort Jefferson and its story, there are two groups whose eyes light up at mention of the Dry Tortugas. They are marine biologists and ornithologists—the fish and bird men (and women).

Alexander Sprunt, Jr., "Blizzard of Birds: The Tortugas Terns," *National Geographic,* February 1947

**DRY TORTUGAS NATIONAL PARK | FLORIDA**

..................................................................................

Fort Jefferson, a four-tiered, six-sided fort composed of more than 16 million bricks and once defended by 1,000 guns, rises from the heart of the Dry Tortugas (on Garden Key, in the lower Florida Keys). Built in the 1840s and 1850s, it was designed to provide an important year-round anchorage, to discourage piracy, and, further, to protect shipping in the Gulf of Mexico and serve as an "advance post" for the security of the Gulf Coast.

**BIG BEND NATIONAL PARK | TEXAS**

For 118 miles, the storied Rio Grande flows along the southern
edge of the Chisos Mountains, slicing through bedrock in Big Bend
National Park (in Santa Elena Canyon, opposite), where it makes a
big turn, or "bend," to the northeast, then continues east-southeast.
The 800,000-acre park is a scenic and ecological jewel, home to
more than 1,200 species of plants (including prickly pear cactus,
backdropped by Pulliam Ridge, above), 450 species of birds,
50 species of reptiles, and 70 species of mammals. From 1964 to
1971, Apollo astronauts visited Big Bend four times to study its
geology in preparation for their visits to the moon.

# BLUE RIDGE MOUNTAINS

I HAD LEARNED FROM JIM HUTCHINS that he and Monroe Thomas swapped frequent letters containing their views on Milton and Shakespeare, original poems, and disquisitions on the relative merits of log cabin and modern consolidated-school education. Against the latter Monroe Thomas launched his philippics in the gentlest of voices:

"Our schools have lost touch with our people. The consolidated schools are bee-hives of industry, pouring an imposing number of subjects through their pupils' ears, but our children have their heads and hearts turned away from the land where they will have to live and work and build their homes. They know nothing about their land and heritage. They cannot name the wild flowers and plants, much less make use of them."

He showed me poems about the woods he could no longer visit. One phrase of his struck: "The old homecrafts are like hunted animals, creeping deeper and deeper into the hinterlands."

Malcolm Ross, "My Neighbors Hold to Mountain Ways,"
*National Geographic,* June 1958

**BLUE RIDGE PARKWAY | NORTH CAROLINA AND VIRGINIA**

The ancient Appalachians layer themselves in blue ethereal light during a sunset over Pisgah National Forest, in North Carolina. The Blue Ridge Parkway (from where this photo was taken, near Cold Mountain, which was made famous in Charles Frazier's 1997 Civil War novel of the same name) runs 469 scenic miles along forested crests from Great Smoky Mountains National Park to Shenandoah National Park.

# JOSHUA TREE

GEN. GEORGE PATTON'S SOLDIERS called it the place God forgot. Training for terrible work here in 1942, they went desperately thirsty; their skin blistered and cracked. They pretended to kill, and a few died; then they went away and won battles in North Africa.

But this place was never forgotten by God, only by California. Until recently this desert in the southeastern third of the Golden State was considered its wasteland: no endless beaches, no surf, no redwoods, no grand agriculture, no incandescent cities. It was just the blazing desolation you had to cross to get from Los Angeles to Las Vegas, the blank space on the map that denies Arizona the sea.

That's changed, dramatically. After two decades of work started by a small band of people who loved a land that others scorned, huge chunks of the California desert have been added to the systems of protection we use to honor our most precious landscapes. Two national monuments—Joshua Tree and Death Valley—have been upgraded to national parks. The 1.4-million-acre Mojave National Preserve, previously a Bureau of Land Management scenic area, has been added to the National Park System. And 69 new wilderness areas have been created. In one sweeping bill called the California Desert Protection Act of 1994, Congress tripled federal park and wilderness acreage in this part of the state to a grand total of 9.2 million acres—a patchwork almost as large as Massachusetts, Connecticut, and Rhode Island combined.

Michael Parfit, "California Desert Lands: A Tribute to Sublime Desolation," *National Geographic,* May 1996

**JOSHUA TREE NATIONAL PARK | CALIFORNIA**

A time-lapse photo of star trails and a twilight sky shows Polaris, the North Star, fixed in its place while neighboring stars make their arcs around it. Standing sentinel, a Joshua tree *(Yucca brevifolia)* is highlighted with artificial lighting. Two desert ecosystems converge in this 790,000-acre park: the high, cool Mojave and the lower elevation Colorado.

**LAKE MEAD NATIONAL RECREATIONAL
AREA | ARIZONA-NEVADA**

..............................................................

An easy quarter-mile-long walk brings hikers to the mouth of
Grapevine Canyon (south of Spirit Mountain), where ancient rock
carvings known as petroglyphs speak silent volumes about the
past. What the petroglyphs—etched between 150 and 800 years
ago—mean exactly remains a mystery today. And thanks to laws
protecting them from defacing and removal, future generations
can ponder—and perhaps solve—this mystery.

*OPPOSITE:*

**CATOCTIN MOUNTAIN PARK | MARYLAND**

..............................................................

Colorful autumn leaves brighten Hunting Creek in this small,
eight-square-mile park in north-central Maryland an hour's drive
from Washington, D.C. It is the site of Camp David, a favorite
retreat for U.S. presidents, so security can be tight here. The park
contains more than 25 miles of compelling hiking and nature trails.
For security reasons, Camp David is unmarked on the maps.

**CAPE HATTERAS NATIONAL SEASHORE | NORTH CAROLINA**

The 198-foot-tall Cape Hatteras Lighthouse greets another sunrise as it stands sentinel over this easternmost mid-Atlantic cape, known as the "graveyard of the Atlantic" for its treacherous conditions. The historic lighthouse was moved in the 1990s—a major engineering feat—from where it had stood since 1870. Otherwise, it would have washed away.

"*There is something infinitely healing in the repeated refrains of nature—the assurance that dawn comes after night, and spring after winter.*"
RACHEL CARSON

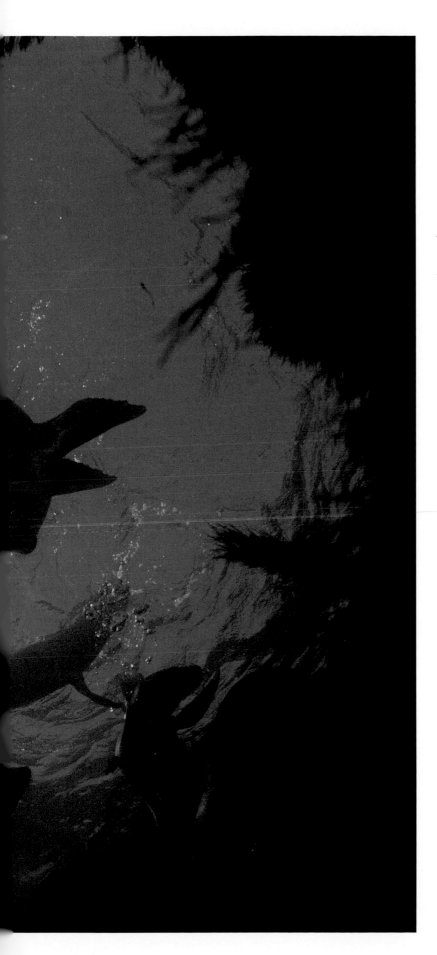

## CHANNEL ISLANDS NATIONAL PARK | CALIFORNIA

First established as a small national monument in 1938 (composed of only Santa Barbara and Anacapa Islands; Anacapa pictured above), the Channel Islands, anchored off the crowded coast of Southern California, exist in relative isolation and serve as a living laboratory for the study of evolution, ecology, marine biology, and island biogeography; hence their reputation as the "Galápagos of North America." Home to more than 150 endemic species, the islands became a biosphere reserve in 1976, which was then enlarged into a five-island national park in 1980—with each new designation gaining the region greater protection. Today, the islands offer a good example of a conservation partnership, as The Nature Conservancy owns and manages three-fourths of Santa Cruz Island, the largest island. Surrounding the archipelago for six miles in all directions, the Channel Islands National Marine Sanctuary protects a vast kelp forest that provides vital habitat for seals, otters, ubiquitous and rambunctious California sea lions (left), and the largest breeding colonies of seabirds in Southern California.

SEQUOIA AND KINGS CANYON NATIONAL PARKS | CALIFORNIA

Sunset over Evolution Lake offers deceptive warmth before a cool
evening settles onto the High Sierra, the mountains John Muir
called the "Range of Light." No roads cross this park east to
west, so rugged is its topography, so sacred its beauty.

# HARPERS FERRY

PROBABLY FEW IN HARPERS FERRY had ever heard of Osawatomie Brown. Certainly they had no cause to suspect a "land and cattle buyer" who came unobtrusively to the Ferry in the summer of 1859.

He called himself Issac Smith, and he rented the Kennedy farm, across the river in Maryland. Nor did the townspeople heed other strangers who drifted in and joined him there, hiding in the farmhouse attic during daylight.

Yet what John Brown and his followers were to do at Harpers Ferry a few months later flickered over the Nation like heat lightning before a distant storm.

Historians have long argued why he chose to strike at Harpers Ferry. Obviously, it held weapons, offered natural hiding places, and lay close to Free State sanctuary in the North. Some, however, say that John Brown's heart leaped at the sheer setting—the rivers tumbling through the cleft in the mountains. Harpers Ferry, only 60 miles by road from the Nation's Capital, was to be his bastion from which to start a general slave insurrection throughout the South.

Volkmar Wentzel, "History Awakens at Harpers Ferry,"
*National Geographic,* March 1957

## HARPERS FERRY NATIONAL HISTORICAL PARK
### WEST VIRGINIA

Nestled at the convergence of the Potomac and Shenandoah Rivers, Harpers Ferry bears witness to stunning scenery—"placid and delightful . . . wild and tremendous," wrote Thomas Jefferson—and profound moments in American history. Here in 1859 John Brown and his men made their raid to end slavery, and alarmed a nation. And here, only three years later, in 1862, Confederate Gen. Thomas "Stonewall" Jackson captured 12,500 Union troops in the largest single surrender of the Civil War. Today, the town's historic district includes a boardinghouse, blacksmith shop, and dry goods store in 19th-century motif, as well as the fire engine house where John Brown was captured by Robert E. Lee, then a Union army colonel before he joined the Confederacy.

**VIRGIN ISLANDS NATIONAL PARK** | U.S. VIRGIN ISLANDS

A family snorkels off St. John Island in an area famous for its warm beauty on land and in the sea. Such bright natural features contrast with the islands' dark past: a history of slavery that ended here in 1848. Seventy years later the United States purchased the islands from Denmark for $25 million. By the mid-1900s, many influential Americans—primarily Laurance Rockefeller, son of John D. Rockefeller, Jr.—sought to make the area a national park, and did so with their great philanthropy, buying 60 percent of St. John Island and gifting it to the National Park Service.

*OPPOSITE:*

**PU'UHONUA O HONAUNAU NATIONAL HISTORICAL PARK** | HAWAII

On the western coast of the Big Island of Hawaii, on a beach once reserved for Hawaiian royalty, wooden statues and other structures—some original, some re-created—speak of two storylines: one about chiefs and other royalty who rested here; the other about life in Hawaii after contact with Europeans. Pu'uhonua o Honaunau, "place of refuge," also sheltered wrongdoers who were condemned to death. Visitors today can hike a two-mile trail and watch contemporary Hawaiians demonstrate traditional crafts.

**GLEN CANYON NATIONAL RECREATION AREA | UTAH**

Impounded as a reservoir behind the controversial Glen Canyon Dam, on the Colorado River, Lake Powell rises and falls according to snowmelt in the Rocky Mountains—and the demands of millions downstream who want water for agriculture, electricity, and drinking. While boating and hiking can be great fun (as in Reflection Canyon, pictured here), many critics of the dam complained that its proponents knew the cost of everything and the value of nothing.

## FROM THE ARCHIVES

# HALEAKALA

HAWAII'S GODDESS OF FIRE, Madame Pele, may live and spew lava regularly at Kilauea Volcano on the Big Island, but it's said that Haleakala Volcano on the island of Maui marks the site of the epic quarrel between Pele and her sister Namakaokahai. The slopes of Haleakala bear the scars of this battle, and also tell the legend of the demigod Maui, whose mother complained that the days were too short for her to dry her clothing. "Maui slowed the sun down in its track by lassoing its rays and impeding its progress," says Charles Kaupu, a *kumu hula* (revered hula master). "He gained a promise that the sun would slow down to allow his mother to dry her *kapa* (bark cloth). It was a good teaching tool for children to help explain the division between seasons."

The sun plays a vital role in the Haleakala experience today, as park visitors head to the crest of the 10,023-foot peak each morning to witness sunrise behind the spectacular summit chasm. Daybreak can be a once-in-a-lifetime thrill, or a bitter wake-up call for the unprepared: Freezing predawn temperatures are common in winter months; warm clothing is a must, even in summer.

David Swanson, "Haleakala: Hawaii's House of the Sun," *National Geographic Traveler,* March 2009

### HALEAKALA NATIONAL PARK | HAWAII

Among the many memorable experiences not to miss on the popular island of Maui is greeting sunrise atop Haleakala volcano, 10,000 feet above sea level. It was here, legend says, that the demigod Maui captured the sun and released it on one condition: that it move more slowly across the sky to make the days longer, richer, better. The 38-mile drive up to here (in the predawn darkness) is in itself a big adventure. Visitors climb above the clouds and might be lucky enough to watch a crescent moon go down as the sun rises and the air warms. Be certain to stock up with food and water before going. Park rangers lead nature walks and half-day hikes from the summit, as well as programs on the night sky. This park can also be enjoyed along the island's southeast coast in the Kipahulu rain forest, with its wondrous waterfalls and freshwater pools, a lush counterpart to the high dry volcanic summit and caldera.

## CAPE COD NATIONAL SEASHORE | MASSACHUSETTS

"Let the sea set you free," say the people of Cape Cod, where the lonely remains of a pier on Herring Cove Beach (opposite) contrast with well-tended sailing boats in busy Provincetown Harbor (above). Some 20,000 years ago a massive glacier dropped its overburden of sediment and rock here, leaving behind a long curving moraine, like an arm reaching into the Atlantic, its hand in a fist. Outwash plains and large boulders (called erratics) also testify to an icy past. While much of the peninsula today has been developed, Cape Cod National Seashore protects open beaches, salt marshes, freshwater wetlands, and scattered woodlands. The relentless Atlantic Ocean pounds away every day, some days more than others, and while setting one free, it also shows no mercy. Many structures have been moved inland over the years, including the historic Highland Light and the Nauset Light. Many more will need to be moved, scientists predict, as sea level rises and storms intensify.

# FIRE ISLAND: THEN & NOW

LESS THAN THREE HOURS FROM Manhattan, this mostly undeveloped, quiet, almost vehicle-free expanse of beach, sand dunes, forest, and wetlands offers a near-total contrast to the noise and bustle of metropolitan life. A unique mix of wilderness, recreation, and private communities, Fire Island has long symbolized escape for city dwellers seeking a quiet place to relax, as well as serving as a rewarding destination for nature enthusiasts eager to explore its varied habitats.

Fire Island is a 32-mile-long barrier island paralleling the southern coast of New York's Long Island. Averaging less than a mile in width it's bounded on the north by bays, on the south by the Atlantic Ocean, and on the east and west by inlets separating it from other islands. The island can be reached only by car at its eastern and western ends; the island's road network is limited to small sections of the island, with no public roads through the main part of Fire Island, and even bicycle use is restricted in many areas. Ferries, water taxis, and private boats provide alternative means of transportation.

Fire Island National Seashore, established in 1964, stretches along 26 miles of the island. (It also includes a 613-acre historical site on the mainland of Long Island, donated to the park in 1965.)

The national seashore's most unusual attribute may be the 17 communities encompassed within its boundaries.

Mel White, *Complete National Parks of the United States*

1939

**FIRE ISLAND NATIONAL SEASHORE | NEW YORK**

......................................

A 32-mile-long barrier island less than three hours from Manhattan, Fire Island parallels the southern coast of Long Island. While reachable by boat and ferry, most of the island is closed to car traffic.

# FROM THE ARCHIVES

# CANYONLANDS

BUT THIS MAZE TRIP WAS SPECIAL. We climbed over sandy hillocks and found ourselves in cactus gardens abloom in lavenders, limes, and creams. Stone shapes like stetsons, boots, and Indian heads loomed on our skyline.

I was in a rock world, and I knew from an earlier visit with Dr. William Lee Stokes, Professor of Geology at the University of Utah, that it was virtually all sandstone. "Even the Arabian Peninsula can't match this country for quantity of sand, though most of it here is stabilized in stone," Dr. Stokes said. "Winds and rains dump the loose sand into canyons, and the rivers carry it downstream, keeping this basin from becoming a mass of dunes."

His geological imagery kept coming back to me, and now in Horse Canyon I suddenly saw the monolithic sandstone all around me as separate bits, attached to each other, grain by grain, in the time frame of the infinite.

Rowe Findley, "Realm of Rock and the Far Horizon," *National Geographic,* July 1971

**CANYONLANDS NATIONAL PARK | UTAH**

Nine days after signing the Wilderness Act in September 1964, President Lyndon Johnson signed the bill creating Canyonlands National Park, a wondrous region of the Colorado Plateau known for its three districts: Island in the Sky, the Needles, and the Maze. Five miles above its confluence with the Green River, near the eastern boundary of the park, the Colorado River doubles back on itself in what geologists call an "entrenched meander," appearing from above like a water snake or an Escher painting. Commonly known as "the loop," this section of river is flanked by ramparts of exquisitely layered sedimentary rock up to 500 feet high. The park is bordered to the west by a portion of Glen Canyon National Recreation Area, and to the east and south by the Bureau of Land Management's Canyon Rims Recreation Area.

"We need another and wiser and perhaps more mystical concept of animals."

**HENRY BESTON**

**ASSATEAGUE ISLAND NATIONAL SEASHORE**
**MARYLAND AND VIRGINIA**

..................................................

Roughly 37 miles long, yet never more than a mile wide, Assateague Island runs along the outer coasts of Maryland and northern Virginia and is best known for its white sand beaches and wild ponies. Back in the 1950s this idyllic island was zoned for a private resort community—more than 5,000 lots sold—until the Ash Wednesday Storm of 1962 halted the plans and made the entire scheme too risky.

# CHAPTER FOUR

# GETTING

REDWOOD NATIONAL
PARK | CALIFORNIA
..............................
Redwoods up to 350 feet tall
thrive in the "fog-drip" forests
of Northern California, where
fog accounts for roughly one-
fourth of the precipitation the
stately trees require.

*it* RIGHT

# Getting It Right
## 1967–1980

---

*"Do you want to know who you are?*
*Don't ask. Act! Action will delineate and define you."*
### THOMAS JEFFERSON

Maybe it was horse sense. Or something in the cosmos. Or simple good luck. Regardless, the National Park Service chose the right ranger in 1969 when they sent George Wagner to the new North Cascades National Park. A seasoned ranger who had worked with horses in both Rocky Mountain and Grand Teton National Parks, Wagner could tie a diamond hitch, write a speeding ticket, speak on the feeding and breeding ecology of bison and elk, quote Wallace Stegner and Bernard DeVoto, tell a good joke, and listen with a keen ear. Raised and educated in Colorado, he loved and embodied the American West, where a handshake sealed a deal. "The Park Service had nothing in the North Cascades when I arrived there," he said. "No buildings, no personnel, no equipment, no presence

**GOLDEN GATE NATIONAL RECREATION AREA**
**CALIFORNIA**

A man hang glides over Golden Gate National Recreation Area, a noncontiguous assemblage of lands in and around San Francisco that comprise 19 separate ecosystems, provide home for more than 1,200 species of plants and animals, and offer dozens of ways to recreate, from horseback riding to bicycling, hiking, and, yes, quietly soaring above it all.

at all. Nothing. I was a lone ranger, in a way. My office space was my hat."

Wagner's colleagues and friends at Grand Teton National Park were sad to see him go. At Wagner's farewell party before he departed for North Cascades, one old-time rancher admitted that while he still didn't like the way Grand Teton had been established—a "snake act," he called it—he had to admit one thing: Honest and trustworthy Wagner had earned his esteem. Others chimed in, and paid their respects, said their goodbyes. Some of George's fellow rangers recalled the Wednesday nights they would all square-dance at the family-friendly Cowboy Bar, where Wagner would gently put his six-month-old daughter, Lora, under the bar, wrapped in blankets, her head on a pillow, as she slept through the live music and foot stomping. Another recalled the time they had lunch at the Wort Hotel, and one ranger left his hat behind. When he went back to get it, it was gone. It turned up a week later, in the parking lot outside park headquarters, riddled with bullet holes. They told stories about the local one-eyed sheriff and his deputy; and President John Kennedy, who'd vacationed in the park and befriended them all, talking late into the night and wanting to hear stories because his older brother Joe, lost on a bombing mission over Europe in World War II, had been a seasonal park ranger. Others recalled that Alan Simpson, a fiercely intelligent man who would one day serve Wyoming in the U.S. Senate, had found in Wagner a good trail companion to match his wit and aw-shucks manner.

Everything was changing then. Sock-hops had become sit-ins. "Revolution" no longer meant the "rpms" in a Chevy or a Ford; instead it referred to America's youth protesting racial inequality and the Vietnam War. While the 1960s were a tumul-tuous decade, no single year rocked America more than 1968: Bobby Kennedy and Martin Luther King, Jr., gone; the U.S. Navy intelligence ship *Pueblo* captured by North Korea; Richard Nixon winning the pres-idential election by the narrowest margin since 1912. Then the Beatles began to unravel. And Atlantic Richfield discovered vast amounts of oil in Alaska's Prudhoe Bay. The year's coda, however, was both sobering and beautiful. During the Christmas holiday, Apollo 8, carrying three astronauts, orbited the moon and returned with startling images of earthrise over the lifeless lunar surface. Around the world people asked: Are we alone? Why are we here? What are we to do with this beautiful planet?

**MARBLES | LINCOLN HOME NATIONAL HISTORIC SITE**

Abraham Lincoln's sons and their friends must have played marbles often; archaeologists have found the beautiful rounded stones in every lot in the Springfield neighborhood where Abraham and his wife, Mary, raised their children from 1844 until 1861.

MEN DIE, DREAMS LIVE ON. In his final days back in 1930, Stephen Mather, confined to his bed, had whispered to Horace Albright, "Cascades . . . cas-cades . . . cascades . . ." Albright thought Mather was referring to a waterfall in an existing park. He wasn't. Mather's dream was to bring the spectacular northwest corner of Washington state, the North Cascades, the so-called American Alps, into his growing family of national parks. It finally happened in 1968, the year that changed America. California's Redwoods National Park came into the fold that same year.

Gone were the days when a national park could be carved from preexist-ing federal lands, or when a bill to establish a park sailed through Congress unimpeded. For lumbermen, redwoods were gold. To leave them standing was absurd and unthinkable. Yes, John Muir said, unthinking lumbermen were the problem. "Any fool can destroy trees. They cannot run away; and if they could, they would still be destroyed—chased and hunted down as long as fun or a dollar could be got out of their bark hides."

Beginning in 1901, separate groves gained protection through private dona-tions. The 1963 discovery of the world's tallest trees by a team of explorers enlisted by the National Geographic Society created strong national inter-est, and a growing desire to protect redwoods. That same year, University

*OPPOSITE, TOP:*

**GEORGE WAGNER | GRAND TETON NATIONAL PARK**

Park ranger George Wagner stands next to an experimen-tal "snow plane" used for winter ranger patrols.

*OPPOSITE, BOTTOM:*

**RANGER HAT | NATIONAL PARK SERVICE**

From 1886 until the creation of the National Park Service in 1916, the U.S. Army Cavalry patrolled the national parks. Soldiers wore a stiff, wide-brimmed hat made of felt that became an iconic part of the standard-issue NPS uniform.

of California zoologist A. Starker Leopold, the eldest son of Aldo Leopold, father of the new American land ethic, headed a scientific committee that issued the Leopold Report, stating, "The major policy change which we would recommend to the National Park Service is that it recognize the enormous complexity of ecological communities and the diversity of management procedures required to preserve them."

By 1964, California state parks contained a total of 50,000 acres of virgin redwoods, thanks in large part to the Save the Redwoods League, founded in 1918 and led until 1940 by Newton Drury, who then would become director of the National Park Service until 1951. Many private philanthropists also played valuable roles, including, once again, Rockefeller. They had saved the largest and tallest remaining trees, what the League called "cathedral-like groves . . . stretching back into the centuries and forging a noble link with the past." Most of these groves occupied river flats and nearby benchlands, and made a good start. But after a stormy winter toppled or undercut hundreds of large redwoods, it became apparent that without saving upslope trees, redwood ecosystems could fail. An intact forest can absorb heavy rains and strong winds, a ravaged or compromised forest cannot.

The problem became a simple yet vexing one: If the oldest, tallest trees were already saved, why worry about the others? Saving a few trees here and there as monuments to size was a much easier argument than saving entire forests as a nod to ecology. Preservationists called for a national park. Lumber companies countered that creating Redwood National Park would put them out of business; besides, they said, the proposed park areas were too cool and damp to attract tourists. The Sierra Club pointed out that the roughly $200 million needed to save a stretch of redwoods along a single creek was a fraction of the cost of a single trip to the moon or a stretch of new interstate. Was walking on the moon more important than saving the greatest trees on earth? "History will think it most strange," proclaimed a *Sierra Club Bulletin,* "that Americans could afford the Moon and $4 billion

PEOPLE IN THE PARKS

# GEORGE B. HARTZOG

The son of a cotton farmer, George B. Hartzog had to drop out of college when his father fell ill. He worked at a gas station and studied law at night. As the seventh director of the NPS (1964-1972), he ushered the National Historic Preservation Act through Congress and made the NPS relevant to urban America with his Bring Parks to the People and Summer in the Parks programs. He appointed the first female, the first African-American, and the first Native American park superintendents. He helped craft early legislation that allowed for the withdrawal of millions of acres of new national parks in Alaska. Interior Secretary Stewart Udall said Hartzog was "a consummate negotiator" who won "most of his arguments with members of Congress, Governors and Presidents." ■

**NORTH CASCADES
NATIONAL PARK**
WASHINGTON

..................................

Lying entirely within the
national park, the Picket
Range is only about six miles
long yet contains more than
20 peaks over 7,500 feet in
elevation.

*BELOW:*
**CENTENNIAL STAMP**
YELLOWSTONE

..................................

In 1972 the U.S. Postal Service helped celebrate the
centenary of Yellowstone—
America's, and the world's,
first national park—with a
commemorative stamp that
depicted Old Faithful geyser.
Annual visitation to America's national parks that year
reached 163 million (at 231
NPS units across the nation).

airplanes, while a patch of primeval redwoods—not too big for a man to walk
through in a day—was considered beyond its means."

CREATIVE COMPROMISE gave birth to Redwoods and North Cascades National
Parks in 1968. Nobody was entirely happy; some jobs survived, some trees
survived. Money, it seemed, would always be tight. Only twice in its history,
in the early 1930s, with FDR's New Deal, and again from 1956 to 1966, during
Mission 66, was the National Park Service flush. The future of the parks lay
in the hands of one Congress after another that always had higher priorities
elsewhere. Yet to adequately save entire biological systems, Congress needed
to provide the NPS with enough land to begin with, and enough money to follow
through with proper, professional management. This was true from Jackson
Hole to the Everglades to the redwoods, where the parks were, at best, attractive fragments of the original America—sad testimonies to the political limits
imposed on complete conservation.

Could entire ecosystems be saved anywhere? Throughout the 1970s, America struggled to heal itself. First came Earth Day, followed by the Clean Air
and Clean Water Acts, the National Environmental Policy Act, the Marine
Mammal Protection Act, and, most remarkable of all, the Endangered

National Parks Centennial
U.S. 8c
Old Faithful, Yellowstone

**MARTIN VAN BUREN HOME
NEW YORK**

Near Kinderhook, New York,
the home of Martin Van
Buren, the eighth U.S.
president (1837-1841),
is one of many stops on the
NPS travel itinerary Discover
Our Shared Heritage:
American Presidents.

Species Act—its political and economic weight not to be felt for another 20 years. Yellowstone celebrated its centennial in 1972. On October 27 of that year, Gateway and Golden Gate National Recreation Areas were established in the hearts of two of the world's greatest cities: New York and San Francisco. Rich and poor alike could now ride a bus or a subway to their local national park and spend an afternoon learning with a ranger. This was a dream come true for California congressman Phillip Burton, who for years had fought for "parks for the people, where the people are." New national monuments, historic sites, seashores, lakeshores, preserves, and other sites entered the system each year—a dozen in 1974 alone. Among them, Big Cypress and Big Thicket, America's first two national preserves, both ecological treasures bursting with biodiversity; plus Clara Barton, John Day Fossil Beds, Martin Van Buren, Tuskegee Institute, and Cuyahoga Valley. Would the Park Service be able to adequately manage them all?

**WHEELCHAIR | CLARA BARTON NATIONAL HISTORIC SITE**

Clara Barton (1821-1912), founder of the American Red Cross, spent the last 15 years of her life in Glen Echo, Maryland. Among the many items on display at her former home is a three-wheeled chair used by the American Red Cross.

*OPPOSITE:*

**IOTA PHI LAMBDA MEMBERS | TUSKEGEE INSTITUTE NATIONAL HISTORIC SITE**

Members of Iota Phi Lambda, an African-American professional and businesswomen's sorority, stand proudly before a statue depicting Booker T. Washington removing the veil of ignorance from the eyes of the black slave.

*"I may be compelled to face danger but never fear it."*

## CLARA BARTON

Such an influx of new sites was not unusual. Ten years earlier, Park Service director George B. Hartzog, described by NPS historian Richard West Sellars as a "politically astute lawyer and Park Service veteran," had succeeded Conrad Wirth with expansionist zeal and, according to Sellars, "capitalized on the momentum of President Lyndon Johnson's Great Society to expand the national park system." This continued through Nixon's first term. "Overall, between 1961 and 1972 (the year Hartzog's directorship ended), a total of eighty-seven units came into the system." The clarion call was "Parkscape U.S.A. . . . to complete for our generation a National Park System by 1972."

⸺◦◦◦◦⸺

AFTER THREE YEARS at North Cascades making friends and establishing a fair but no-nonsense Park Service presence, Wagner returned to Rocky Mountain to work with horses. It beat paperwork. Everywhere rangers were specializing, a trend that would only increase. "I resisted specialization my entire career,"

**TOURISTS | YELLOWSTONE NATIONAL PARK**

.....................................

Visitation to the national parks exploded with the vast expansion of the American middle class after World War II. By the time Yellowstone turned 100, in 1972 (right), it was often crowded with summertime visitors.

*BELOW:*

**THE MONKEY WRENCH GANG | 1975**

.....................................

Former National Park Service ranger Edward Abbey (1927-89) wrote many good novels, but none like *The Monkey Wrench Gang*, wherein four ecosaboteurs conspire to bring down the Glen Canyon Dam.

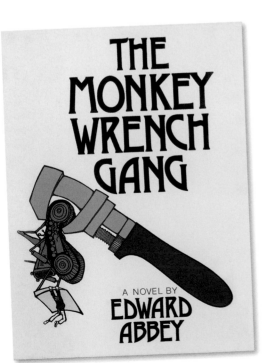

Wagner said. "Rangers should range," wrote Edward Abbey in his best-selling memoir, *Desert Solitaire,* about his life as a ranger in Utah's Arches National Monument (before it was a park). Abbey spent some time on the back of a horse; mostly he hiked and ran rivers. "There will always be one more river," he wrote, "not to cross but to follow." For two summers he lived in a trailer at Balanced Rock and went about his duties as he saw fit: watching clouds, counting cottontails, inspecting rocks, hiking trails, scrambling up cliffs, getting lost and finding himself, and befriending a rattlesnake that lived under his trailer. Every so often Abbey talked to visitors. One hot summer day a survey crew arrived in their government jeep, dusty and thirsty. The head engineer, described tongue-in-cheek by Abbey as "a very dangerous man," said they were planning to build a fancy new road through the area so ten, twenty, thirty times as many tourists could visit Arches. Abbey wrote, "He stared at me intently, waiting to see what possible answer I could have to that. 'Have some water,' I said. I had an answer all right but I was saving it for later. I knew I was dealing with a madman." Abbey continued, "Several years after the little episode of the gray jeep and thirsty engineers, all that was foretold has come to pass . . . Where once a few adventurous people came on weekends to camp for a night or two and enjoy the taste of the primitive and remote, you now find serpentine streams of baroque automobiles pouring in and out."

When does access become excess? Who are the national parks for, and in what numbers? Imagine Carnegie Hall filled to capacity, every seat taken. Do we then crowd the aisles and back walls? No, we invite people to the next performance. Progress and paradox are twin heads of the same serpent, Abbey warned. His comic eco-novel *The Monkey Wrench Gang,* published in 1975, portrays the Hoover and Glen Canyon dams on the Colorado River not as great engineering feats but as abominations, defilements—and the reservoirs behind them not as lakes but as evaporation ponds and silt traps. John Muir would have agreed. The 1976 presidential election that ushered Jimmy Carter into the White House set the stage for the National Park Service to achieve what it never had or could or would in the lower 48: the protection of wild lands and indigenous cultures on a full ecosystem scale.

All eyes turned north.

**PORCUPINE | NOATAK NATIONAL PRESERVE**

........................................

A porcupine stands its ground along a river in Noatak National Preserve, in northwestern Alaska. Roughly 90 percent (5.8 million acres) of this preserve is designated as wilderness. The centerpiece of the preserve, the Noatak River, flows out of the Brooks Range, the northernmost mountain range in the world.

———◆———

"SCALE AND DIVERSITY FOIL all who try to simplify Alaska," wrote NPS historian William E. (Bill) Brown. "Its immense and ceaseless grandeur numbs the mind,

# GRANT-KOHRS RANCH

The Grant-Kohrs Ranch of Deer Lodge, Montana, once a ten-million-acre cattle empire, is today a national historic site (established in 1972) that commemorates the role of cattlemen in American history, beginning in the 1850s. "They were a rugged set of men, these pioneers," observed Conrad Kohr in 1913, "well qualified for their self-assumed task. In the pursuit of wealth a few succeeded and the majority failed . . . The range cattle industry has seen its inception, zenith, and partial extinction all within a half-century. The changes of the past have been many; those of the future may be of even more revolutionary character." On display at the site are the many museum artifacts pictured here. ■

**RANCH ARTIFACTS**
**GRANT-KOHRS NATIONAL**
**HISTORIC SITE, MONTANA**

......................................

1. Matchbook; 2. Cattle horns; 3. Cattle prod; 4. *Doc Savage* magazine; 5. Fur gloves; 6. Cowboy boots; 7. Lariat.

**RANCH ARTIFACTS**

**GRANT-KOHRS NATIONAL**

**HISTORIC SITE, MONTANA**

...........................................

8. Chaps; 9. Indiana Pioneers ribbon; 10. Cattle boot; 11. Doll; 12. Decorative stool with cattle horn legs; 13. Spurs.

glazes the eye, and plagues the writer who would describe it. The intellect cannot close the suitcase on this subcontinent. Always a spare peninsula or archipelago or coastal plain dangles out after the sweaty struggle to buckle the straps." Added conservationist Margaret "Mardy" Murie, winner of the Presidential Medal of Freedom and the first woman graduate of the University of Alaska (Fairbanks), "We cannot foretell the future, but we can give a nod toward it by putting this last treasure of wild country into an interest-bearing savings account. In the long view—all Alaska needs to do is be Alaska."

The discovery of oil in Prudhoe Bay prompted Alaska Natives to band together to preserve their rights, resources, and economic opportunities before an oil pipeline was built and they found themselves economically disadvantaged. There would be no Trail of Tears in Alaska. A 1971 settlement act gave Alaska Natives 44 million acres and one billion dollars to invest wisely, with each Native a shareholder in his or her Native corporation. Embedded in this was a mandate for another act, one to conserve lands of "national interest." The Park Service sent a task force of rangers, scientists, historians, and anthropologists to research possible new parks. "This was our chance to save America," Brown said. "Many of us had been born too young to fight in World War II; that rankled us. Now was our time."

It was exciting, and challenging. While Alaska's congressional delegation could see the value of having a Yellowstone or Yosemite, they feared something much larger and economically crippling, and spoke as if this lands act might be an attempted robbery, of sorts. It boiled down to money and jobs—nothing new. Former Park Service director Newton Drury countered, "Surely the great United States of America is not so poor we cannot afford to have these places, nor so rich that we can do without them." Hundreds of environmental organizations formed the Alaska Coalition, inspired by the triumvirate of Congressman John Seiberling of Ohio, Secretary of the Interior Cecil Andrus, and President Jimmy Carter.

"In Alaska we have the opportunity to learn from our past mistakes," said Edgar Wayburn of the Sierra Club. Niagara Falls, Lake Tahoe, the Florida

A caribou antler rests on autumn tundra in Gates of the Arctic National Park, one of eight national parks in Alaska.

**PEOPLE IN THE PARKS**

# JIMMY CARTER

"I see this simple little bill lying on the table here," President Jimmy Carter said when he sat down to sign the Alaska National Interest Lands Conservation Act of 1980. Those around him laughed. The bill's creation had been anything but simple. It represented years of artful compromise that saved 97 million acres of new parks and refuges, protected 25 free-flowing rivers, more than doubled the acreage in the National Park System, and tripled the size of the designated wilderness system. Carter added, "We should always change the world in which we live with great care . . . We have nothing more precious than life itself, nothing more valuable to us than health." At the 25-year-celebration of the lands act, in 2005, Carter was welcomed back to Alaska as a hero. ∎

Keys—these were the places that got away, the parks that never were. Since
the early 1900s, no national park of any considerable size had been created
without local opposition. Yet after one or two generations, few, if any, people in
those areas wanted the parks dissolved. In Grand Teton, the most contentious
national park ever established in America, many grandsons and granddaugh-
ters of former naysayers now appreciated the park and its many gifts.

Volumes of Alaska testimony poured in; the debate raged on. "If Congress is
unable to act," warned Cecil Andrus, "President Carter and I will." And they
did. Late in 1978 Andrus withdrew 110 million acres. Then Carter used the
1906 Antiquities Act to establish 56 million acres of new national monuments. Many Alaskans were incensed. They berated Carter in the press
and burned him in effigy in Eagle, on the Yukon River. In Glennallen, a
Park Service plane was torched. John Cook, director of the National
Park Service in Alaska, told his rangers to stay cool and always be honest. Inspired by T. R. and FDR, Carter had thrown down the gauntlet,
saying that national parks transcended local prejudices and special
interests. Congress hammered out a bill, and in 1980 Carter lost his
reelection bid to Ronald Reagan. In the 11th hour of his presidency,
however, Carter signed the great Alaska lands act of 1980 that created
more than 100 million acres of new national parks, preserves, and
wildlife refuges. The parks' names themselves sounded like poetry:

Gates of the Arctic, Kobuk Valley, Wrangell–St. Elias, Kenai Fjords, Lake Clark, Katmai, and Glacier Bay. Wrangell–St. Elias National Park and Preserve, the largest in the U.S. National Park System, was six times the size of Yellowstone. And Mount McKinley was tripled in acreage and renamed Denali National Park and Preserve, in honor of the Native Athabascan name meaning "the high one."

"This was our chance to do things right," said Brown, "and—by God—we did. We saved Alaska. We saved America."

**DALL SHEEP | DENALI NATIONAL PARK AND PRESERVE**

The only species of wild white sheep in the world, Dall sheep inhabit the higher contours of the Outer Range, in Denali National Park, and on occasion come downslope and cross the park's single dirt road, giving visitors a great thrill.

As HIS CAREER DREW TO A CLOSE in the late 1980s, Wagner received an offer from an old friend: Would he like to be chief of interpretation at Denali? Wagner said yes, and fell in love with Denali, and with the incomparable Sandy Kogl, manager of the Denali Sled Dog Kennels. "I traded horse sense for dog power," he said with a robust laugh, "and had many wonderful times in the backcountry with the entire Milky Way overhead, the immense winter stillness broken only now and then by the howls of wolves, and the dogs answering, like distant cousins from long ago." ■

# GREAT LANDS

## 1967–1980

NATIONAL PARKS CAME to America's cities in the later half of the 20th century, by which time nearly two-thirds of the units in the National Park System were historical and cultural sites, many within a short distance of millions of people. The first Earth Day occurred in 1970, followed quickly by passage of many of America's most important environmental laws: the Clean Air Act, Clean Water Act, and Endangered Species Act, among others. Yellowstone, our first national park, celebrated its centennial in 1972. And eight years later, in early December 1980, President Jimmy Carter signed a great lands act that established more than 100 million acres of new national parks, preserves, and wildlife refuges in Alaska.

**BISCAYNE NATIONAL PARK | FLORIDA**

.........................................................................

Boca Chita Lighthouse greets visitors to Biscayne National Park: 90 percent water and home to many threatened and endangered species, including the West Indian manatee, and five species of sea turtles

FROM THE ARCHIVES

# APPALACHIAN TRAIL

ON AUGUST 5, 1948, a certain shoe manufacturer missed the chance of a lifetime. He should have been on a bleak mountaintop to greet a tired but happy hiker in ragged footwear.

The weary walker was Earl V. Shaffer of York, Pennsylvania. On that day he reached the summit of Mount Katahdin, in central Maine.

Thousands had preceded Shaffer to that rocky pinnacle. But he had just walked more than 2,000 miles over the full length of the Appalachian Trail. He had left Mount Oglethorpe, Georgia, on April 4. He was the first, so far as the record shows, to traverse that Olympian footpath in a single continuous journey.

I asked the redoubtable hiker how many pairs of shoes he wore out in four months of "hoofing it" over rock and rubble, on leaf mold and pine needles, through swamp and stream bed.

"One pair of boots lasted the whole way," he replied. "But they were in tatters at the end."

On his long walk Shaffer's durable shoes tickled the mountain backbone of the eastern United States. He spent 123 nights on the trail, several of them in fire towers. Traveling alone, he averaged 17 miles a day.

The only "enemies" Shaffer met were two copperheads and a rattlesnake.

Andrew H. Brown, "Skyline Trail from Maine to Georgia," *National Geographic,* August 1949

**APPALACHIAN NATIONAL SCENIC TRAIL | GEORGIA TO MAINE**

A runner makes quick work of a stream crossing on the Appalachian Trail, a 2,185-mile-long path along the weathered spine of the Appalachian Mountains through 14 states, from Georgia to Maine. Three to four million visitors hike part of the trail each year.

**NORTH CASCADES
NATIONAL PARK
WASHINGTON**

.........................................

Mount Shuksan (9,131 feet high) makes a memorable reflection in North Cascades National Park, less than three hours from Seattle. The park contains more glaciers (more than 300) than exist in all the rest of the contiguous 48 states. The park also boasts 75 mammal species in 20 families, including the grizzly bear, banana slug, Columbian black-tailed deer, Douglas squirrel, and the sure-footed mountain goat (opposite).

FROM THE ARCHIVES

# NORTH CASCADES

OUT IN THE NORTHWEST CORNER of the country, up against the Canadian border, lies a sparsely peopled land of snowy mountains and forest solitudes—the North Cascades wilderness, in Washington State. If Congress this session completes action on a bill already passed by the Senate, the choicest part of it will become our newest national park.

What is it like? Last summer I went to see, and now I can report that it is like nothing else—unique in itself—though at times it seemed composed of about equal parts of Alps, virgin forest, and the easy informality of the old West.

As we roamed this peak-studded wilderness, National Park Service planner Neal Butterfield and I felt as if we were peeling back generations to a time when the West was new. We felt in touch with our pioneer heritage as we trekked the high trails of the Cascades with old-time packers and their horses. We sensed it in the scent of saddle leather and campfire, in the clang of metal-shod shoe on rock—and in every one of our saddle-weary bones at night.

Nathaniel T. Kenney, "The Spectacular North Cascades,"
*National Geographic,* May 1968

*"Patience, patience, patience, is what the sea teaches. Patience and faith. One should lie empty, open, choiceless as a beach—waiting for a gift from the sea."*
**ANNE MORROW LINDBERGH**

**REDWOOD NATIONAL PARK | CALIFORNIA**

Best known for its tall and ancient trees, this park also contains prairies, oak woodlands, wild rivers, and nearly 40 miles of pristine coastline, such as Enderts Beach, warmed here by sunset.

## FROM THE ARCHIVES

# REDWOODS

THE STORY OF NORTH AMERICA'S COAST REDWOODS is one of nearly heedless destruction, belated appreciation, and vigorous conservation.

These magnificent trees, among the tallest on Earth, once covered 2 million acres along the Pacific coast of California and Oregon. Their valuable timber made them targets for uncontrolled logging in the 19th century—an activity that, while more regulated in the 20th century, still resulted in the loss of 96 percent of the old-growth forest that once stood as one of the most splendid and awe-inspiring ecosystems on our planet.

Much about a redwood is impressive, especially its size (up to 370 feet) and life span (up to 2,000 years—its scientific name *sempervirens* means "living forever"). A redwood cone, the size of an olive, contains 60 to 120 seeds, and one tree may produce ten million seeds.

(And what, as everyone asks, is the tallest redwood? In 2006 a new champion was discovered deep in the backcountry of Redwood National and State Parks, at 379 feet high.)

Yet redwoods can thrive only in a limited range of environmental conditions. They can't grow directly along the coast because they are vulnerable to salt spray. Yet they must be close enough to the ocean that fog can condense on them on summer nights, providing vital moisture during the dry season.

Mel White, *Complete National Parks of the United States*

**REDWOOD NATIONAL PARK | CALIFORNIA**

Together with California's Del Norte Coast, Jedediah Smith, and Prairie Creek Redwoods State Parks, Redwood National Park protects roughly 45 percent of all remaining coast redwoods. Because of this, the United Nations designated the parks a World Heritage Site in 1980, and an International Biosphere Reserve in 1983.

**ROSS LAKE NATIONAL RECREATION AREA | WASHINGTON**

Seen from Desolation Peak, the double summits of Hozomeen
Mountain (8,071 feet and 8,003 feet) dominate the northern reaches
of Ross Lake, adjacent to North Cascades National Park. Jack
Kerouac spent the summer of 1956 manning a fire lookout atop
Desolation Peak, a setting for his novel *Desolation Angels*.

# FROM THE ARCHIVES

# ANDERSONVILLE

IN EARLY 1864, AT THE HEIGHT of the Civil War, the Confederacy built a prison in southwestern Georgia to hold captured Union soldiers. Officially called Camp Sumter but later commonly known as Andersonville Prison (for a nearby small town), the compound because infamous for the terrible conditions endured by the inmates, resulting in the deaths of nearly 13,000 men by the close of the Civil War.

Today's Andersonville National Historic Site encompasses the location of the prison as well as a national cemetery and the National Prisoner of War Museum, which commemorates the sacrifices of all American prisoners of war in conflicts such as World Wars I and II, Korea, Vietnam, and the Middle East.

The original Camp Sumter was a 16.5-acre site surrounded by a wooden stockade. With a small creek flowing through its center, it was designed to house a maximum of 10,000 prisoners of war. A smaller fence was erected inside the tall stockade; any prisoner who crossed this "dead line" to approach the outer wall was shot by sentries stationed in guard posts around the stockade.

Crowded conditions quickly led to a 10-acre expansion of Camp Sumter. In August 1864 Andersonville housed some 32,000 prisoners, all suffering from malnutrition, disease, and the heat of a Georgia summer.

Mel White, *Complete National Parks of the United States*

**ANDERSONVILLE NATIONAL HISTORIC SITE | GEORGIA**

The Camp Sumter military prison at Andersonville existed for only 14 months in 1864-65, yet its reputation for suffering, death, and disease burned deep into the American consciousness. It began as a stockade designed to hold 10,000 Union Army prisoners captured by Confederate forces; it eventually held 32,000 at one time, 45,000 total, many of them wounded and starving. Nearly 13,000 men died here and were buried in a nearby cemetery.

**CUMBERLAND ISLAND NATIONAL SEASHORE | GEORGIA**

Georgia's largest and southernmost barrier island, Cumberland
Island is a refuge of pristine maritime forests (opposite), undeveloped beaches, and tranquil marshes—9,800 acres of which are
designated as wilderness. Here visitors can turn their calendars
back 100 years to a simpler time: to days filled with birdsong and
nights rippled with the starry spiral of the Milky Way. At certain
times fierce winds might reshape the barrier dunes; at other times
the entire island holds its breath, windless, while calla lilies (above)
slowly unfold. Among the more noteworthy species that rely on
this and other barrier islands are wood storks, piping plovers,
least terns, gopher tortoises, manatees, and sea turtles.

Baby American alligators enter the world in Big Cypress, a 720,000-acre preserve that borders the freshwater prairies of Everglades National Park and helps to save a larger percentage of the entire Everglades ecosystem.

# BIG THICKET

"IT'S THE BOTANICAL DIVERSITY that makes the Thicket so special," she said. In a soft east Texas drawl, pleasant on the ear, she explained that the Big Thicket was an ecotone—a biological crossroad, where a wide variety of plant communities meet and intermingle: plants found in the Appalachians and plants found in the tropics, even plants characteristic of the deserts.

Geraldine counts seven distinct types of plant associations in the Thicket, with thousands of species. There are 40 species of orchids, 26 of ferns, and four of North America's six genera of carnivorous plants.

On that first trip and others Geraldine showed me cactus and yucca, sphagnum moss and sticky-leaved sundew, huge cypress and great oaks with resurrection fern growing like pale-green fur along the branches. She pointed out graceful but voracious pitcher plants. A lizard had fallen into one, she said, and "the plant's enzymes had devoured him down to the skeleton."

Once along Village Creek she stopped and smelled the jasmine-scented air. "I spent my childhood in virgin woods," she said. "Our house was in a beech-magnolia forest, and nearby was virgin longleaf pine, and we'd walk in there in the afternoon—it was cool, there among the big trees and the wildflowers. I can just close my eyes and smell the air, and I'm back home again."

Don Moser, "Big Thicket of Texas,"
*National Geographic,* October 1974

**BIG THICKET NATIONAL PRESERVE | TEXAS**

In 1974, the National Park Service acquired two new national preserves: Big Thicket in southeast Texas and Big Cypress in southwest Florida, both on the same day, October 11. Described as the "American Ark," Big Thicket was specifically established to protect its rich array of plant life: more than 1,000 species of ferns and flowering plants in nine separate land units and six water corridors.

## JOHN DAY FOSSIL BEDS NATIONAL MONUMENT | OREGON

Ever since 1864, when Thomas Condon, a missionary and amateur geologist, unearthed fossils in this remote semi-desert scrubland of east-central Oregon, paleontologists have been digging into the past here, finding fossils of plants and animals dating back from 5 million to 44 million years ago. The entire monument rests within the John Day River Basin, the longest undammed tributary of the Columbia River. At night, Western pipistrelle bats hunt moths over the desert scrub (above), while during the day the Painted Hills invite the eye to every horizon (opposite), colored by spring flowers. Elk, coyotes, and voles frequent the area, as do butterflies, reptiles, and fish.

*"The growth of our science and education will be enriched by new knowledge of our universe and environment, by new techniques of learning and mapping and observation."*

**JOHN F. KENNEDY**

CANAVERAL NATIONAL SEASHORE | FLORIDA

On the southern tip of this barrier island, the John F. Kennedy Space Center honors the president who in 1961 committed America to put a man on the moon by the end of the decade, which we did in July 1969.

**EBEY'S LANDING
NATIONAL HISTORICAL
RESERVE | WASHINGTON**

......................................

"If Rebecca, and the children, and you were all here," wrote pioneer Colonel Isaac Neff Ebey to his family back in Missouri in 1851, "I think I could live and die here content." "Here" being on the northern neck of Puget Sound's Whidbey Island, at the site of today's 19,333-acre Ebey's Landing National Historical Reserve that includes two nearby state parks.

# NEW RIVER GORGE

ADVENTURE, HISTORY, AND BEAUTY merge in West Virginia's New River Gorge, where the stream at the bottom (not new, and in fact possibly one of the oldest river systems on Earth) lies more than 1,000 feet below the plateau through which it runs. Most famous for its white-water boating opportunities, the New River offers a variety of paddling options.

The upper river or the southern section, as the New runs northward, features rapids rated Class I–III separated by long pools. Thus, it is suitable for canoeists and other boaters with medium experience level. However, the famed "lower gorge" below Thurmond includes rapids rated to Class V and is appropriate for skilled paddlers only. Many commercial outfitters offer guided river trips, which provide the less experienced an opportunity to enjoy the gorge. Only primitive camping is available within the park. Five campgrounds are located along the river, and one sits atop a ridge; all are reachable by gravel roads.

The hard sandstone cliffs of New River Gorge have made the park one of the most popular rock-climbing locations in the country. More than 1,600 climbing routes have been established, most rated 5.9 and higher.

Mel White, *Complete National Parks of the United States*

**NEW RIVER GORGE NATIONAL RIVER** | WEST VIRGINIA

Don't be fooled by the name. The New River, rugged and white water, is among the oldest rivers in North America. The gorge hosts more than 1,400 rock-climbing routes, plus challenging and fun rafting. President Jimmy Carter signed the legislation to create this national river "for the purpose of conserving and interpreting outstanding natural, scenic, and historic values and . . . for the benefit and enjoyment of present and future generations."

# SAN ANTONIO MISSIONS: THEN & NOW

**1913**

**SAN ANTONIO MISSIONS NATIONAL HISTORICAL PARK | TEXAS**

Under threat from French settlers spreading out from Louisiana, Spain sent missionaries north from Mexico in the late 1600s and early 1700s to build a series of walled, medieval communities. According to the National Park Service, "Spanish missions were not churches. They were Indian towns, with the church as the focus, where, in the 1700s, the native people were learning to become Spanish citizens."

BEGINNING IN 1718, Spain built five mission compounds along the San Antonio River with the goal of converting native people to Catholicism and making them Spanish citizens. France was asserting its power to the east in Louisiana, and Spain felt the need to reinforce its cultural and military presence in what is now Texas. Each mission was made up of a church, living quarters, storerooms, and other outbuildings set within defensive walls (guarding against Indian attacks). Outside the mission walls, crops were planted and animals were kept, making the sites self-sustaining communities as much as religious centers.

Perhaps the most well-known of the five missions is the Mission San Antonio de Valero, begun in 1724. Known today as the Alamo, it starred as the scene of a dramatic 13-day siege in 1836 in the Texas Revolution. Located in downtown San Antonio, it is preserved as an independent shrine of Texas history.

The other four missions, scattered along the river south of the central city, make up San Antonio Missions National Historical Park. Each site includes a church that still functions as an active Catholic parish, holding regular services. Visitors are welcome inside the churches during park hours, except during special events such as weddings and funerals.

Mission San José, the largest of the missions, has been most fully restored, including its gristmill and defensive wall. Visitors with time to visit only one mission should choose San José, known as the Queen of the Missions. (The park visitor center is also located adjacent to San José.)

Mel White, *Complete National Parks of the United States*

**KENAI FJORDS NATIONAL PARK | ALASKA**

A sea kayaker navigates through icebergs discharged off the face of
a tidewater glacier. The nearby city of Seward opposed the creation
of this park until tourists arrived by the tens of thousands.

**KOBUK VALLEY NATIONAL PARK | ALASKA**

The ancient rhythms of wind and water give character and grace to the Kobuk River Valley, on the northern edge of the boreal forest in the far northwestern corner of Alaska. Here congregations of barren-ground caribou of the Western Arctic caribou herd (the largest of 14 major caribou herds in Alaska) cross the river at Onion Portage (above) during their annual migration between summer calving grounds and winter feeding grounds. A short distance downriver, the Great Kobuk Sand Dunes, the largest Arctic dunefield in North America, catch the low Arctic light. Samples from peat bogs reveal that the dunes have been here for at least 33,000 years. Together with two smaller nearby dunefields, the sand dunes cover about 200,000 acres.

**LAKE CLARK NATIONAL PARK | ALASKA**

A horned puffin, one of two species of puffin that nest in Alaska, prepares to take flight off a sea cliff. Members of the auk (alcid) family, puffins lay one egg at the end of deep, cliff-top burrows.

### NOATAK NATIONAL PRESERVE | ALASKA

. . . . . . . . . . . . . . . . . . . . . . . . . . . . . . . . . . . . . . . . . . . . . . . . . . . . . . . . . . . . . . . . . . . . .

"The Noatak is the largest mountain-ringed wilderness river basin in North America," National Park Service historian William E. (Bill) Brown wrote. "It has a scope, a sweep as awesome and unforgettable as the desert or the Great Plains." The centerpiece of this preserve, the Noatak River, runs 450 miles west from the Brooks Range through canyons and moraines and into the Bering Sea. "This is intimate country—old, and softened by time," wrote river guide Karen Jettmar. "I can visualize the mammoths and bison of old, browsing in the grassland steppe while most of North America lay ice-covered. In every direction I see distant mountains beyond the miles of tussocky tundra, grassy swales, thaw ponds, lakes and creeks."

At 13.2 million acres, Wrangell–St. Elias National Park and Preserve is the largest unit in the National Park System. Glaciers of many kinds reside here, such as rock glaciers (opposite). In the heart of the park stands the Kennecott Copper Mine (above, with Mount Black-burn), regarded by many as the most photogenic historic mine in Alaska.

## FROM THE ARCHIVES

# WRANGELL-ST. ELIAS

I CAN'T GET OVER THE FEELING that I'm the last person on earth. Or maybe the first. In the sweep of an eye from Chitistone Pass I see not one human sign, only snow-packed peaks, gray stone ridges, and, far below, a broad green valley. Through the valley winds a river born from a dripping glacier.

It is mid-June, but at 5,822 feet I slog through patches of snow. A grizzly has left its signature in them as well, long claw marks fringing oval paw prints. Like me, it is moving from the Wrangell Mountains to the St. Elias, for Chitistone Pass marks the meeting point of these two ranges in southeast Alaska.

I prepare to yield to that humpbacked monarch, the griz, just as the nation has yielded to nature in these rugged mountains. In 1980 Congress established Wrangell-St. Elias National Park and Preserve and ordered that it remain essentially undisturbed. The result is our biggest national park—13.2 million acres, an area larger than New Hampshire and Vermont combined.

Noel Grove, "Alaska's Sky-High Wilderness," *National Geographic,* May 1994

STEPHEN J HUSKEY • ROBERT E RYAN •
KENDALL • MICHAEL L HINO • JOSE MA
HARD C DORITY • DAVID L GINN • HARVEY D
CALVIN A NORRIS • ERROL L KENT • ERNEST J MON
JOHN D SHEWMAKE Sr • JAMES R PANTALL • JERRY
CHARLES D DODD • DAVID W WOODS • LERO
Jr • DAVID J WATSON • RICHARD R KAPSHA • JAMES
N H JAMES Jr • JOHN M CLARK • JAMES
WILLIAM E SUMMERS • FRANCIS J KLASSEN • HOWARD M
ARNOPLOSKY • ROGER D DAVENPORT • ERIC
THOMAS J PUFF • DAVID ATOIGUE GORTON • ROBE
R LANGE • BRADFORD M GRAHAM • CHARL
HAROLD D BOWEN • DANIEL
SON • CARTER
SAU

# VIETNAM MEMORIAL

FOR THESE GIs, COMING HOME had not been like John Wayne had promised.

They had gone to Vietnam filled with images of John F. Kennedy and Hollywood movies, and they did their duty, even though few of these images matched the muck and the moral confusion they found in Indochina.

After 12 months they were put on an air-conditioned airplane with pretty stewardesses, and suddenly the war was over. "Wash up," one returning veteran's mother had said. "Your welcome-home dinner is ready." He looked down at his hands. Mud from Vietnam was still under his fingernails.

No one wanted to hear what the vets had been through. People who saw them in uniform might spit, shout "Murderer," or ask, "How come you were stupid enough to go?" Or, if you'd arrived home blind or missing an arm or a leg, someone might come up and say, "Served you right."

Thus, many vets carried powerful and disturbing feelings that were buried deeper and deeper as the war became old news to other Americans.

For Jan Scruggs—wounded and decorated for bravery when only 19 years old in 1969—the feelings surfaced in March 1979 after he saw *The Deer Hunter,* an emotional movie about combat in Vietnam. "I'm going to build a memorial to all the guys who served in Vietnam," Scruggs told his wife. "It'll have the names of everyone killed."

Joel L. Swerdlow, "To Heal a Nation,"
*National Geographic,* May 1985

**VIETNAM VETERANS MEMORIAL | WASHINGTON, D.C.**

Etched in a black granite wall, the names of more than 58,000 Americans who lost their lives in the Vietnam War make a simple yet profound statement. Millions of loved ones trace their fingers over these names; they leave dog tags, photos, mementos, flowers, prayers, and tears.

CHAPTER FIVE

# REACHING

WAS A DRUM MAJOR
PEACE AND RIGHTE

SE I LOVE AMERICA. I SPEAK OUT AGAINST
ETY AND SORROW IN MY HEART, AND
E DESIRE TO SEE OUR BELOVED
L EXAMPLE OF THE WORLD.

IF WE ARE TO HAVE PE
RATHER THAN SE
OUR TRUE,
WE

# the *the* PEOPLE

INJUSTICE ANYWHERE IS A THREAT TO JUSTICE
CAUGHT IN AN INESCAPABLE NETWORK OF
A SINGLE GARMENT OF DESTINY. WHAT
ONE DIRECTLY, AFFECTS ALL IND

**MARTIN LUTHER KING, JR., MEMORIAL | WASHINGTON, D.C.**

..........................................................................................

The sculpted image of civil rights leader Dr. Martin Luther King, Jr.
(1929-1968), towers over twilight visitors in West Potomac Park.

# Reaching the People 1981–2016

———◆———

*"To the lover of pure wildness Alaska is one of the most wonderful countries in the world."*

**JOHN MUIR**

On a summer day in coastal Alaska, a luxury cruise ship navigated up an inlet and slowly approached a massive tidewater glacier—an imposing wall of ice rising from the sea, one mile across, 250 feet high. Black-legged kittiwakes pinwheeled off their cliff nests and landed on pieces of floating ice around the ship. Harbor seals swam about, ever watchful. A bald eagle perched on a tall pinnacle of ice that appeared ready to break away from the glacier at any minute and collapse into the sea. Sunlight danced off unnamed, unclimbed mountains in all directions. As the ship inched closer and turned abeam of the glacier,

**CRUISE SHIP | GLACIER BAY NATIONAL PARK AND PRESERVE**

Visitors on a small expedition tour boat approach the tidewater face of Margerie Glacier, where it ends in upper Tarr Inlet, and calves tall columns of ice into the sea. Three hundred years ago, this inlet—and the entire 70-mile-long bay—was buried under a single massive glacier up to 4,000 feet thick.

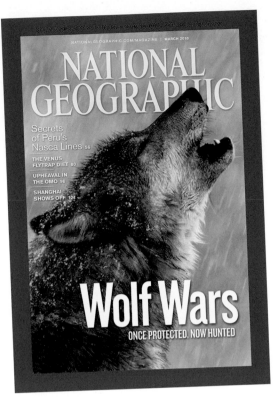

**"WOLF WARS"** | *NATIONAL GEOGRAPHIC* MAGAZINE

.....................................

some 2,000 passengers watched in amazement, a few from inside warm lounges and staterooms, others from outside, standing at the rail, speechless, lost in the ice age. This wasn't Kansas anymore. It wasn't Orlando either, or Chicago, or even Seattle, where 20,000 years ago glaciers filled all of today's Puget Sound. This was Glacier Bay National Park, here and now, wild nature on an outrageous scale, the greatest show on earth. This was Alaska, the Africa of America.

The glacier cracked and popped. A piece of ice fell from the uppermost parapet and hit the sea with a sound like a cannon shot. Everybody startled, then wanted more. One woman had tears in her eyes. She'd dreamed about coming to Alaska her entire life, and now she was here, with her grown son and daughter, and just in time, before the cancer took her. Another passenger set up an easel to paint the glacier. Many snapped photographs. A group of blind ladies, seated on the aft deck, thrust small tape recorders into the air whenever the glacier made a sound. Park naturalists patrolled the decks and quietly answered questions about glaciers, whales, birds, and bears, but gave no formal talks. They'd done that earlier in the day. It was time now to let the ancient ice speak.

———◆———

NOT A DAY GOES BY in America when somebody isn't charmed, inspired, or educated in a national park. The parks are pleasuring grounds, but also, and just as important, they are proving grounds, places to let science and truth have their say. Never was this more hotly tested than in Yellowstone in the final two decades of the 20th century, first with fire, then with wolves.

June of 1988 broke high temperature records across America. Low water on the Mississippi River restricted barge traffic, and the Alabama National Guard hauled water to people whose wells ran dry during the worst drought since 1934. NASA scientist James Hansen testified to a Senate committee that "the greenhouse effect has been detected, and it is changing our climate now."

Would this be our legacy?

Amid such dire news, few people noticed when a series of June fires began to burn in the world's most famous national park. By mid-July, Yellowstone was ablaze. Vice President George H. W. Bush ended a backcountry fishing trip when flames approached his camp near the park's eastern boundary. Another fire burned a backcountry ranger cabin and forced rangers to dive under an emergency shelter as flames danced overhead. Lewis Campground was closed. Grant Village was evacuated (twice). Fire swept through Norris Geyser Basin,

and the smoke became so thick that drivers used headlights. While dramatic and frightening, of equal interest (and debate) was Yellowstone superintendent Bob Barbee's decision—backed by his director—to let the fires burn as long as safely possible.

Fire is destructive, yes. It's also historic and regenerative. Scientists said the Yellowstone ecosystem needed periodic fires to remain healthy, and Barbee believed them. Critics (many of them local business owners) said a national park badly scarred by fires would be unpopular the following year. They were wrong. In 1989, Yellowstone received 2.6 million visitors, the highest number in the 1980s. Plant growth was unusually lush that year. Burned pine bark proved nutritious for elk. Grizzly bears did well. Aspen seedlings appeared throughout the park's burned areas. And what of the park's whitebark pine forests, nearly a quarter of which had burned? Scientists set up 275 study plots to monitor new growth. By 1995, according to the Park Service, "whitebark pine seedlings had emerged in all the plots."

That same momentous year, 1995, after decades of often rancorous debate and 160,000 letters to Congress, plus ceaseless lobbying, education, outreach, lawsuits, and delays, a miracle happened. A small group of wolves from western Canada were released into Yellowstone. "An ocean of elk and bison awaited them," wrote Montana author and conservationist Rick Bass.

**WOLVES | YELLOWSTONE NATIONAL PARK**

The 1995 reintroduction of wolves into Yellowstone National Park (after a 70-year absence) became a landmark event in ecological thinking and wildlife management in the United States. The entire world took notice, and is still watching.

"Upon the wolves' return, so sudden was the transformation, so quick the reparations, that it seemed a marvel that the landscape—brittle and fractured as it had become in the absence of even that one species—had been able to hold together as well as it had for those seventy or so years . . . The elk were no longer encamping in any one spot like feedlot animals, and the restored riverbanks served as nesting and feeding habitat for songbirds of different hues."

Yellowstone was alive again, singing once more to the howls of its primary predator, a song that once filled all the world's high latitudes. As Bass concluded, "There is color in the land again. Or perhaps it was always there, like a pigment in the soil, but was simply rendered imperceptible for a while."

---

THROUGHOUT THE FINAL two decades of the 20th century, the National Park System grew in exciting ways, both in depth and breadth, acknowledging past presidents with the Harry S. Truman and Jimmy Carter National Historic sites, and the original, pre-agriculture American heartland with the Tallgrass Prairie National Preserve. To achieve this required a public-private partnership with the Nature Conservancy in the Flint Hills of Kansas. The Korean War Veterans Memorial, in Washington, D.C.'s West Potomac Park, honors America's "sons and daughters who answered the call to defend a country they never knew and people they never met." It depicts full-size, battle-weary soldiers in helmets and ponchos, rifles at the ready, walking through the rain. A testimonial letter from a Korean woman who was an infant at the time said, "This is a story of an old woman and the war. The soldiers who came from far away to help South Korea saved our family and saved my life. All the happiness and love I now enjoy came from the blood of the sacrificed and the tears of the terrified. Thank you. My life was dependent on you. Your bravery, your courage should never be forgotten."

When Doug Cuillard, chief of interpretation at Alaska's Denali National Park and Preserve, was chosen to be superintendent at the National Park of

# SANDY DAYHOFF

Environmental education specialist Sandy Dayhoff did more than touch lives, she changed lives. Consider Maria Thomson, a divorced immigrant with two small children, who met Sandy when she visited Maria's son's elementary school and shared the magic of the Everglades. The same thing happened to Maria's daughter. Twenty years later, all three—mother, daughter, and son—are park rangers. "To be a national park ranger," Maria says, "is not just a job, it is a mission, a mission to protect special places and help people to connect to them. It is a wonderful opportunity to make a difference. Every time we touch a heart we can change a life, the same way that many years ago, a ranger changed my life." ∎

FIELD TRIP | JIMMY CARTER NATIONAL HISTORIC SITE, GEORGIA

Kindergarten students visit the boyhood farm of James Earl "Jimmy" Carter to learn how farming, church, and school shaped the values that Carter took to the White House and beyond.

*BELOW:*

TRUMAN'S WORLD CLOCK HARRY S TRUMAN NATIONAL HISTORIC SITE

Engraved onto the front of this world clock are the initials "HST," for Harry S. Truman. The 33rd U.S. president had a deep interest in world events and loved to surround himself with clocks.

American Samoa, he needed to learn new skills—among them, how to sit Samoan-style. When the Samoans met to discuss important matters, they crouched on their haunches, like baseball catchers, and remained so positioned for hours, talking. No chairs. No sofas. No shoes. To sit Western style, flat on the ground and showing the bottoms of your feet, was an insult to your neighbors. The Samoans took pity on Cuillard though; they could see he was a good man trying his best with his stiff and creaky North American knees. So they allowed him to sit flat on the ground, legs straight, and to cover his feet with a blanket.

A flurry of new parks, preserves, and historic sites established in 1988 and 1992 showed two presidents, Ronald Reagan and George H. W. Bush, in their final White House years focused on legacy as well as the economy, perhaps inspired, or haunted, by Teddy Roosevelt. Opportunities to save vast, untouched landscapes were gone. By the mid-1990s, the United States had half a million miles of roads—in its national forests alone. Every year an area equal to the size of Yellowstone National Park, fell under asphalt, concrete, or other development. Miami, Phoenix, Las Vegas, Seattle, and other cities grew with remarkable speed. As did the stock market. Amid all this, the California Desert Protection Act of 1994 re-designated Death Valley and Joshua Tree from national monuments (established in the 1930s) to national parks. It also enlarged them to include new features, and established Mojave National Preserve. Death Valley became the largest U.S. national park outside Alaska. The act saved

# MANZANAR

AFTER JAPAN ATTACKED THE U.S. NAVY at Pearl Harbor, a fear of Japanese Americans led to their internment by the U.S. government in places the National Park Service today calls "sites of shame." The most well known camp was California's Manzanar, preserved today at Manzanar National Historic Site. The stories here are sad and inspiring: of people finding their dignity, doing crafts, playing baseball, making friends, all behind barbed wire, while some internees had sons and brothers who fought bravely in a U.S. combat unit in France. A hand-painted teakettle (opposite) left at the Manzanar Cemetery came with a note: ". . . wanted to bring some sunshine, flowers and beauty to this sacred site. We are so sorry that this tragedy ever happened and are here to pay our respects." ■

**MANZANAR ARTIFACTS**
**MANZANAR NATIONAL**
**HISTORIC SITE, CALIFORNIA**

.......................................

1. Relocation authority
badge; 2. Shogi pieces;
3. Japanese-American soldier
dog tag; 4. Painted shells;
5. Camp footwear.

⑥

⑦

⑧

⑨

⑩

**MANZANAR ARTIFACTS**
**MANZANAR NATIONAL**
**HISTORIC SITE, CALIFORNIA**

6. Teakettle; 7. Baseball mitt; 8. Origami; 9. Japanese-American G.I. Joe; 10. Heirloom kimono basket; 11: Manzanar graduation ring.

⑪

a total of 3.6 million acres and designated 69 new wilderness areas. Off-road enthusiasts called it the California Desert "Restriction" Act, fearful that they'd no longer be able to ride their machines wherever they wanted. "Moments after President Clinton signed the Desert Protection Act into law this week," wrote John Canalis in the *Los Angeles Times,* "four baby tortoises and their older brother slowly made their way across his desk to greet him. The tortoises belong to Whittier [California] residents Elden and Patty Hughes and are known around Capitol Hill as some of the cutest lobbyists in town." Scientists had found what most people already knew: Tortoises do poorly in the company of all-terrain vehicles. And so the reptiles of California, like the wolves of Yellowstone, found a reprieve from the heavy hand of man.

**ELK HIDE PAINTING**
**SAND CREEK MASSACRE**
**NATIONAL HISTORIC SITE,**
**COLORADO**

Artist Eugene Ridgely depicts the Sand Creek Massacre, where Chief White Antelope stands by an American flag—and a white peace flag—as militiamen attack a peaceful camp and kill more than 250 Indians.

*OPPOSITE:*

**SAND DUNES | MOJAVE**
**NATIONAL PRESERVE,**
**CALIFORNIA**

Mojave National Preserve features the largest Joshua tree forest in the world and the "singing" Kelso sand dunes, so named because of a low frequency rumble visitors hear when walking the dunes.

*"We must uncenter our minds from ourselves; we must unhumanize our views a little, and become confident as the rock and ocean that we were made from."*

**ROBINSON JEFFERS**

THE NEW CENTURY OPENED with tragedy. Almost 100 years to the day that William McKinley was assassinated and Teddy Roosevelt ascended to the White House (September 1901), the United States came under the attacks of September 11, 2001, when three hijacked commercial airliners were used to strike targets on the ground. Nearly 3,000 people lost their lives, most of them when Manhattan's World Trade Center towers were hit and then collapsed. In an open field in western Pennsylvania, the Flight 93 National Memorial honors the 40 passengers and crew who thwarted a fourth 9/11 attack by forcing terrorists to bring down a commercial airliner that otherwise would have crashed into Washington, D.C., most likely the U.S. Capitol building while Congress was in session. David Larsen, a legendary interpretive trainer and recipient of the Sequoia Award, the highest honorary award for excellence in NPS interpretation, was tasked with the difficult duty of designing the educational component of the memorial. Skilled at connecting hearts and minds to places,

PRESIDENT OBAMA
AND HELEN CHÁVEZ
CÉSAR E. CHÁVEZ
NATIONAL MONUMENT,
CALIFORNIA

..........................................

To sign the executive order to
create a national monument
for labor rights leader César
Chávez, President Barack
Obama traveled west to
Chávez's home and gravesite,
where he also visited his
widow, Helen.

*BELOW:*

ROSIE THE RIVETER
WORLD WAR II HOMEFRONT
NATIONAL HISTORICAL
PARK, CALIFORNIA

..........................................

"You can learn all your civilian WWII history," wrote one
visitor about this Richmond,
California, park that honors
the tens of thousands of civil-
ians—most of them women—
who helped win the war.

his motto was "Let visitors feel—be relevant or become a relic." Inspiration
and learning will follow. He once quoted Loren Eiseley at a meeting of the
George Wright Society: "Life is a series of shooting sparks . . . all the rest is
interpretation." In Pennsylvania, at the Flight 93 National Memorial, Larsen
succeeded in turning tragedy into triumph. He sadly died eight months before
the memorial was opened in September 2011. Since his passing, some 300,000
people have visited the memorial each year.

⸺⸺•❦•⸺⸺

HOW TO MAKE NATIONAL PARKS and historic sites relevant? And equitably
shared by all Americans? More than any time before, the Park Service
reached out to women and minorities with Rosie the Riveter/World
War II Home Front National Historical Park, César E. Chávez National
Monument, and the breathtaking Martin Luther King, Jr., Memorial
in the heart of our nation's capital. New "sites of shame" also came
into its fold, such as Sand Creek Massacre National Historic Site.
Still, imbalances remain. "In the natural realm," stated former Park
Service deputy director Denis Galvin in 2014, "the national park
system is 13 percent rock and ice, only 3 percent wetland. It is pre-
dominantly western . . . There are 100 acres of national park for every
citizen of Alaska, while there are almost 1,000,000 citizens for every acre

of national park in Illinois." How then to make people care for their parks and heritage? How to get them out of their gadgets and into their senses? In 2014, 81 percent of U.S. citizens lived in cities. By 2030, that number is expected to jump to 87 percent. The National Park System Advisory Board recommended that the NPS "engage in large landscape scale conservation, expand connections with urban populations, and develop institutional capacity in the NPS for systems planning and partnerships." In other words, bring the parks to the people.

⎯⎯⎯ ❖ ⎯⎯⎯

THE KEY HAS ALWAYS BEEN partnerships, first with railroads, then with the U.S. Army, auto clubs, chambers of commerce, conservation organizations, and sportsman and education groups, among others. In the more recent past, the Park Service has spearheaded many watershed conservation projects that involved state and local governments and private organizations all over the country, from Chesapeake Bay and the Everglades in the East to hundreds of

**WALKING THE TRAIL OF TEARS | TRAIL OF TEARS NATIONAL HISTORIC TRAIL**

Artwork depicts Cherokee Indians leaving their homeland after passage of the Indian Removal Act of 1830. Other tribes were also removed (more than 45,000 Native Americans total) and forced to walk west to designated Indian Territory, along the 5,000-mile-long "Trail of Tears." Many died.

Hikers negotiate the spine of
Mount Lafayette on the Appalachian Trail. Known locally as
the A.T., the trail is one of the
most popular in the U.S.

places out West. Environmental education in the Everglades alone has reached tens of thousands of children—future decision-makers in Florida. The Rivers, Trails, and Conservation Assistance Program helped 900 communities in a single year to protect more than 300 miles of river and develop 2,000 miles of trails. The Leave No Trace program, offering education in outdoor recreation ethics, has swept the nation and is helping to keep pristine places as they should be. The National Trails System, managed by the NPS and other agencies, protects the Maine-to-Georgia Appalachian Trail, the Trails of Tears in North Carolina and Oklahoma, the Captain John Smith Chesapeake National Historic Trail in Hawaii, and other trails of merit. In 2008, the independent, bipartisan National Parks Second Century Commission released a "visionary report" that called for "dramatic enhancements to the National Park System and the NPS's ability to protect our breathtaking landscapes and historic and cultural treasures." The commission further said the agency must "provide meaningful new opportunities for all Americans—especially young people and diverse communities—to become connected with our shared heritage, and involved to protect it."

The national parks have been the first victims of government shutdowns and yet, not surprisingly, park rangers have remained the positive face of the federal government, admired by young and old, men and women, liberals and conservatives.

Consider Rick McIntyre, a biological technician who has tallied more than 87,000 wolf sightings and hasn't missed a day of work in 15 years. Every morning in June he gets up at 3:15 and drives into Yellowstone to spend another 10 to 16 hours with wolves—watching, listening, sharing. "In college I studied timber management and learned to cut down trees," he says. "Then I discovered national parks, America's greatest invention, greater even than jazz."

He's been passionate about his work ever since.

Overseas, sister parks and partnerships have abounded for decades, with the U.S. National Park Service providing leadership and management training, along with many programs on topics such as techniques for managing visitor use.

PEOPLE IN THE PARKS

# RICK MCINTYRE

By 2016, when the National Park Service turns 100, Rick McIntyre will have worked for the NPS 42 of those years, mostly as a seasonal interpretive naturalist from Padre Island to Denali to Big Bend to Joshua Tree and elsewhere. Since the mid-1990s, he's been a "wolf interpreter" and biological technician in Yellowstone, where he's tallied more than 10,000 pages of field notes and 1,000 public presentations. He studies guitarist Jimi Hendrix for inspiration, always seeking to do things better. His job, as he sees it, is both science and art, and always a privilege. "It's not just knowledge that's going to save the wolf, and save the world," he says. "It's storytelling. In everything I do, I am a storyteller." ∎

The national park idea has grown into myriad expressions of innovative commitment and technological applications to save the best of what we have and who we can be. This is the dream of every ranger: to teach the younger generation the magic, beauty, and healing properties of nature, the power of their own history and stories. To be aware; to see global challenges as golden opportunities. To help map the way through the Clean Energy Revolution as the only future we can afford. The world burns a gigaton (one cubic kilometer) of oil every 45 days. This cannot continue without imperiling a bountiful future. "The world's in a bad way, my man," wrote poet Robinson Jeffers, "and bound to be worse before it mends." That mending can begin with national parks. It already has.

---

**CONGRESSIONAL GOLD MEDAL | TUSKEGEE AIRMEN NATIONAL HISTORIC SITE, ALABAMA**

..................................

African-American members of the 332nd Fighter Group and 477th Bombardment Group of the U.S. Air Force, commonly called the Tuskegee Airmen, were collectively awarded a Congressional Gold Medal in 2007.

**ELWHA DAM | OLYMPIC NATIONAL PARK, WASHINGTON**

..................................

A century after it was constructed in 1910, the Elwha Dam, which destroyed habitat for Pacific salmon, was brought down to great fanfare. Estimated cost of dam removal and river restoration: $350 million.

OVER THE YEARS, the cruise ships that visit Glacier Bay have increased dramatically in size, as has the political and economic might of the cruising industry. Alaska has become the number one cruising destination in the world, and Glacier Bay the jewel in the crown. Still, only two ships per day are allowed into the bay. This prevents crowding and gives each ship the sense of having the bay to itself. In all of Alaska's 34,000 miles of coastline—more coastline than in the entire contiguous United States—Glacier Bay National Park is the only place where the numbers of vessels (cruise ships, tour boats, and private

motorized vessels) are limited. Northbound, the ships often stop in the port town of Ketchikan, Juneau, and Skagway, where passengers hit the jewelry stores, T-shirt shops, and popcorn stands. As many as 10,000 might crowd Juneau's streets during a busy summer Wednesday, when several ships are in town. Glacier Bay is different. It's sacred—a national park, a biosphere reserve, and a World Heritage Site. As such, the Park Service requests that the ships offer no competing activities—no gambling, art auctions, dance lessons, or comedy shows. Nobody sets foot on the land, yet nearly everybody is expectant, excited, and, once at the tidewater glacier, transfixed. Before them, only a quarter mile away, is a window into the distant past. The glacier, 21 miles long, begins high in the Fairweather Range, the snowiest mountain range in the world, and flows all the way down to the sea. Rather than tapering into a melting toe of ice, as glaciers do on land, this one ends in a vertical blue wall rising out of the ocean, tempting the tides of fate.

A hush falls over the ship, as if a sermon were being delivered, the oldest of all, spoken by the Earth itself, what John Muir called "the gospel of glaciers." Nobody asks for this moment of silence. It just happens. Out of awe and respect. A few people stand at the rail, teary-eyed. Others take a long, deep breath, and hold loved ones close. It's their day in their national park—a holy place. ∎

**TORRES DEL PAINE NATIONAL PARK | CHILE**
......................................

Torres del Paine National Park—a "sister park" of Yosemite National Park—embraces stunning mountains, forests, and glacial lakes in the windy Patagonia region. One of 36 national parks in Chile, Torres del Paine reminds people all over the world of the importance of wild places to feed the mind, heart, and soul.

# SACRED PLACES

# 1981–2016

"WHAT MAKES A PLACE SPECIAL," observes author and anthropologist Richard K. Nelson, "is the way it buries itself inside the heart, not whether it's flat or rugged, rich or austere, wet or arid, gentle or harsh, warm or cold, wild or tame. Every place, like every person, is elevated by the love and respect shown toward it, and by the way in which its bounty is received." Thanks to our national parks, preserves, monuments, seashores, historic sites, and other public lands, special places now and yet to come, the journey continues, to look both forward and back and to apply all that's been learned. Can our parks—can our very nature and history—remain sacred, even relevant, in an age of too many gadgets? Today, park rangers and teachers across the country inspire citizens to love and respect their heritage—to receive the bounty with great gratitude, to honor it, and to pass it on.

**TALLGRASS PRAIRIE NATIONAL PRESERVE | KANSAS**

They say you can chase the horizon and never get there on the vast American prairie, nearly all of it plowed under these days. Not so in the Flint Hills of Kansas, where the sun rises and sets over nearly 11,000 primal acres, managed by The Nature Conservancy and the National Park Service.

## FROM THE ARCHIVES

# NATCHEZ TRAIL

THROUGH FORESTS, OVER MOUNTAINS and deserts, across river fords, and around impenetrable swamps, land-hungry pioneers tramped out the trails of North America. The American epic rings with the names of these footpaths that became highroads of civilization: the Boston Post Roads, the Santa Fe and Oregon Trails, El Camino Real, the Wilderness Road—and the Natchez Trace.

Winding between Natchez, Mississippi, and Nashville, Tennessee, the Trace—old French for "a line of footprints"—played a great and turbulent role in America's westward expansion. In weeks of wandering over the 500 miles of frontier road and the modern Natchez Trace Parkway that memorializes it, I crossed and recrossed the paths of men of destiny—above all Andrew Jackson, the dominant hero of Trace history. But I trod, too, in the footsteps of some of our country's greatest roisterers and rapscallions.

I began on a sunny autumn day on the waterfront of Natchez, for that was where most old Trace journeys started. Except for the buffalo and Indians whose hoofs and moccasins beat out the path long before Columbus, most of the early travelers of the Trace arrived in Natchez not by road but by river.

Bern Keating, "Today Along the Natchez Trace,"
*National Geographic,* November 1968

**NATCHEZ TRACE NATIONAL SCENIC TRAIL | MISSISSIPPI**

In the early 1800s, thousands of American pioneers traveled by foot and horse on the Natchez Trace, a well-known trail from Nashville, Tennessee, to Natchez, Mississippi. Visitors today can drive the sinuous 444-mile-long Natchez Trace Parkway, past split-rail fences and beautiful stands of trees, or go more quietly, in the old way, by horse or foot, on four segments of the original trail in Mississippi that total 65 miles.

## STEAMTOWN NATIONAL HISTORIC SITE | PENNSYLVANIA

Through much of the 19th and 20th centuries (especially between 1850 and 1950), railroads played a large role in building modern America, and our dreams of travel. "Even if you're on the right track," said humorist Will Rogers, "you'll get run over if you just sit there." By the 1950s, with the construction of the interstate freeway system and the emergence of diesel-electric engines, steam-powered locomotives themselves ended up just sitting there. The 62-acre Steamtown National Historic Site in Scranton, Pennsylvania (above and opposite) preserves and celebrates that golden age of commerce and travel—the romance of the railroad—when 65,000 steam loco-motives covered more than a quarter-million miles of track across the United States, making us dream of other places.

**KOREAN WAR VETERANS MEMORIAL | WASHINGTON, D.C.**

On the National Mall, 19 realistic stainless-steel statues depict members of the Army, Navy, Marine Corps, and Air Force, who fought in harsh conditions from 1950 until 1953 to evict the military forces of Communist North Korea from South Korea.

In the final choice a soldier's pack is not
so heavy a burden as a prisoner's chains."

**DWIGHT D. EISENHOWER**

## FROM THE ARCHIVES

# AMERICAN SAMOA

A THIRD OF OUR PLANET is Pacific Ocean. Away out in that undulating blueness, 2,600 miles southwest of Hawaii and 1,800 miles northeast of New Zealand, appears the small island known as Ofu. Built of soaring black stone, it is robed in rain forest and further softened by summit mists from which waterfalls spill back down toward the sea.

I lie floating a few feet from shore, fingertips lightly anchored in sand. Inches from the bottom half of my diving mask, long-nose filefish cruise over coral colonies.

I keep the top half of my mask above the water, watching raindrops pock the surface. Beyond, palm fronds sweep over a white beach where Ofu tapers toward the storm-blue spires of its sister isle, Olosega. There is nobody on the shore, only fat coconut crabs clawing their way into fallen coconuts to gorge on the sweet coatings inside. I could stay like this for hours—and do, in one of the newest, most unusual, and least familiar additions to the U.S. National Park System, the National Park of American Samoa. The entrance signs, in Samoan, read *Paka o Amerika Samoa* with the subtitle *Laufanua Fa 'asaoina,* or preserved land.

Samoa itself is said to mean "sacred center."

Douglas H. Chadwick, "The Samoan Way,"
*National Geographic,* July 2000

**NATIONAL PARK OF AMERICAN SAMOA | AMERICAN SAMOA**

Composing 9,000 acres on land and 4,500 acres of coral reefs and ocean spread over four islands, this park offers exquisite snorkeling and hiking, yet receives few outside visitors. The islands are remote: roughly 2,600 miles south-southwest of Hawaii. Yet they're well worth a visit for their more than 900 species of fish, 250 species of coral, and many dazzling birds of the paleotropical forests. The rich Samoan culture is also a treat here.

**CITY OF ROCKS NATIONAL RESERVE | IDAHO**

As civilization expands, open tracts of land shrink. Species vanish.
Silence disappears. The National Park Service now partners with
other organizations to save fragments of the original America,
such as City of Rocks, administered by the NPS and the Idaho
Department of Parks and Recreation. Climbers call it "the City,"
because an early pioneer said that from a distance the rocky
formations looked like modern buildings.

"One of the great dreams of man must be to find some place between the extremes of nature and civilization where it is possible to live without regret."

**BARRY LOPEZ**

# MISSISSIPPI RIVER

FLOWING 2,320 MILES from Minnesota's Lake Itasca to the Gulf of Mexico, the Mississippi River has served as an important transportation corridor, an endlessly varied recreational resource, and an inspiration for an array of art, from Mark Twain's novels to musical theater to folk songs — and continues to do so. Over the past two centuries this fabled waterway has been dammed, channeled, leveed, diverted, polluted, and altered in countless other ways.

Nowhere along its length does the river change more than along a 72-mile stretch north and south of Minneapolis-St. Paul, transforming from a relatively undeveloped and quiet prairie stream to a major commercial waterway. (St. Paul began as the Mississippi's historic head of navigation, the bookend to New Orleans.) In recognition of this uniqueness and the need to maintain the river's resources for all citizens, Congress designated this stretch the Mississippi National River and Recreation Area in 1988 in order to provide it with special protection.

Mel White, *Complete National Parks of the United States*

## MISSISSIPPI NATIONAL RIVER AND RECREATION AREA | MINNESOTA

.......................................................................

Any river that travels more than 2,300 miles north to south is bound to have plenty of character — and stories. The Mississippi is in many ways the heart of America: big, beautiful, hardworking; legendary and still mysterious; portrayed in novels, plays, and songs, yet never fully captured. Near its youthful Minnesota headwaters, it matures from a largely undeveloped prairie stream into a broad boisterous commercial waterway, and here, in a 72-mile stretch north and south of Minneapolis–St. Paul, its uniqueness is protected by the NPS.

**PETROGLYPH NATIONAL MONUMENT | NEW MEXICO**

..............................................................................

Cooperatively managed by the National Park Service and the city of
Albuquerque, this 7,200-acre monument protects more than 20,000
petroglyphs: ancient rock art created between the early 1300s and
the late 1600s. These images and designs carved into the stones'
desert varnish surface—unlike pictographs, which are painted—
often depict people dancing or hunting, or birds, or snakes (above).

*OPPOSITE:*

**NIOBRARA NATIONAL SCENIC RIVER | NEBRASKA**

..............................................................................

The Niobrara River gives little hint of the controversy that surrounded it for decades. Should it be damned or left free-flowing?
The battle ended when 76 miles of the 500-mile-long river were
designated a national scenic river. While most rivers in the heartland
are dammed or sluggish, the Niobrara is rich with waterfalls and
rapids that attract thousands of water lovers every year.

**VIRGIN ISLANDS CORAL REEF NATIONAL MONUMENT**
**VIRGIN ISLANDS**

A school of brightly colored yellow French grunt fish rest along the ocean floor off St. John Island. President Bill Clinton established this 12,700-acre marine monument by executive order.

# LITTLE ROCK HIGH: THEN & NOW

1957

**LITTLE ROCK CENTRAL HIGH SCHOOL NATIONAL PARK | ARKANSAS**

All storms pass, as did the 1950s desegregation conflicts at Little Rock Central High School. On September 26, 1957 (left), federal troops stood armed and ready to escort students into class, if need be. Tensions were high. Decades later (opposite), the high school stands amid more peaceful times, and racial discrimination, while still a sore on the soul of the South, is nothing like it used to be.

IN SEPTEMBER 1957, NEWSPAPER HEADLINES around the world reported events taking place in Little Rock, the capital of Arkansas. Nine African-American students attempted to integrate all-white Central High School, despite opposition by Arkansas Gov. Orval Faubus and other state and local officials to court decisions ordering an end to segregated education. The threat of violence prompted President Dwight Eisenhower to order federal military troops to escort the students, and the "Little Rock Nine" eventually were allowed to attend classes.

What became known as the Crisis at Little Rock was a milestone in the decades-long struggle for civil rights in the United States. The state-federal confrontation is commemorated today at Little Rock Central High School National Historic Site, which encompasses the only still functioning high school within a national historic site.

A visitor center adjacent to the high school presents interactive exhibits on the background and importance of the desegregation crisis, as well as audiovisual programs on the events in Little Rock during the fall of 1957. Rangers conduct programs year-round, although tours of Central High School itself are available only with advance reservation to groups of ten or more.

Mel White, *Complete National Parks of the United States*

## FROM THE ARCHIVES

# CRATERS OF THE MOON

IN THE WEST THE TERM "Lava Beds of Idaho" has always signified a region to be shunned by even the most venturesome travelers—a land supposedly barren of vegetation, destitute of water, devoid of animal life, and lacking in scenic interest.

In reality the region has slight resemblance to its imagined aspect. Its vegetation is mostly hidden in pockets, but when found consists of pines, cedars, junipers, and sagebrush; its water is hidden deep in tanks or holes at the bottom of large "blow-outs" and is found only by following old Indian or mountain sheep trails or by watching the flight of birds as they drop into these places to quench their thirst. The animal life consists principally of migrant birds, rock rabbits, woodchucks, black and grizzly bears; its scenery is impressive in its grandeur.

A glance at a map of Idaho shows that the southern part of the State, lying between Arco and Carey and north of Minidoka, is a vast region labeled desert or rolling plateau.

Although almost totally unknown at present, this section is destined some day to attract tourists from all America, for its lava flows are as interesting as those of Vesuvius, Mauna Loa, or Kilauea.

R. W. Limbert, "Among the 'Craters of the Moon,'"
*National Geographic,* March 1924

**CRATERS OF THE MOON NATIONAL MONUMENT
AND PRESERVE | IDAHO**

Unique in the family of National Park Service units, Craters of the Moon began as a national monument established in 1924 by President Calvin Coolidge. President Bill Clinton enlarged the monument in 2000. Two years later, the expanded portions of the monument became a national preserve, closed to roads and construction but open to hunting. Today, the area is cooperatively managed between the National Park Service and its sister agency, the Bureau of Land Management.

*"This generation of Americans has a rendezvous with destiny."*

## FRANKLIN DELANO ROOSEVELT

**WORLD WAR II MEMORIAL | WASHINGTON, D.C.**

Dedicated to the "Greatest Generation," the World War II Memorial commemorates the 16 million Americans who served in the U.S. military from 1941 to 1945.

## FROM THE ARCHIVES

# AFRICAN BURIAL GROUND

HOWARD UNIVERSITY ANTHROPOLOGIST Michael Blakey confronts the skull of an African man exhumed from the 18th-century African Burial Ground, found during construction of a federal building in lower Manhattan. Blakey's five-year study of the remains of 427 people shows that nearly half died by age 12. All lived hard lives; 75 percent of the men and 65 percent of the women had telltale evidence of torn muscles or fractures caused by carrying heavy loads. One child had two such fractures, dental defects indicating malnutrition or disease, and signs of anemia. "We wondered how this child made it to the age of six," he says.

Many graves held signs of African origin: filed teeth, a woman with 111 glass waist beads, and a coffin with tacks outlining a heart-shaped design, identified as the Ashanti symbol *sankofa,* meaning loosely, "Look to the past to inform the future."

Bill Denison, "Face-to-Face With Slavery's Victims,"
*National Geographic,* October 1997

**AFRICAN BURIAL GROUND NATIONAL MONUMENT**
**NEW YORK**

Visitors pay their respects where some 15,000 captive and freed Africans were buried on a seven-acre site from about 1690 to 1790, when the Dutch disallowed such burials within the walls of New Amsterdam (later New York City). By the early 1800s, the burial site was forgotten. In 1991, construction crews working on a new federal building rediscovered the site. Public outcry called for its preservation and today it hosts a visitor center and a portion of the cemetery that was saved.

**FIRST STATE NATIONAL HISTORIC PARK**
**DELAWARE AND PENNSYLVANIA**

Sunrise warms Woodlawn in Brandywine Valley, a 1,100-acre
tract of upland meadows and woods in Delaware's first national
monument, established in 2013 by President Barack Obama.

# People in the Parks

*"Now I see the secret of making the best persons.
It is to grow in the open air, and to eat
and sleep with the earth."*

## WALT WHITMAN

"I was born to a single mother. She was sick, and we were poor," says 31-year-old Eugenie Bostrom, her voice quavering as she stands before a hundred attendees at a wilderness conference in Albuquerque, New Mexico. "Living just outside Los Angeles, with a constant mountain backdrop in the inconceivable distance; the only camping my family ever did was in shelters, or in living out of our car. We were modern nomads. People without place. With my mother's health failing, she was forced to give up custody. My brother and I were placed in a group home outside of Chicago . . ." Bostrom pauses. The crowd is silent, still. "'Wilderness' was a word I don't think I ever heard until I turned 16. That summer, I applied to be a member

**DC WAR MEMORIAL**
**WASHINGTON, D.C.**

Constructed by the District of Columbia to honor the local men and women who gave their lives in World War I, this open-air Doric structure came into the fold of the National Park Service in 2014.

........................................

Members of a Youth Conservation Corps pose for a photo in the world's first national park. Every year young people have the best summer of their lives working and playing hard, discovering the wonders and delights of nature, and learning how they, like so many before, can contribute to a better world.

of the Yellowstone Youth Conservation Corps, the YCC. It wasn't Yellowstone that intrigued me. I didn't know what Yellowstone was. I had never heard of the National Park Service. My sole understanding of government was through the Department of Child and Family Services. What interested me was that a girl who had left my same Chicago group home a few years prior had participated in the YCC and gone to college. I believed the only way out of this cycle of poverty was to attend college; that's what I wanted most—to break the cycle. It was the summer of 1998."

Bostrom's voice grows steady, strong, almost serene.

"Now, I want to discuss another disenfranchised species: the gray wolf, exterminated from Yellowstone in 1926." She speaks about the 1995 reintroduction, the wolves transported from Canada, and how they were held in three separate acclimation pens for a month before getting set free to work their ecological magic. "I feel like you can see where this is going: A disconnected youth finds a love of nature and her life is changed forever. While that's true, it's not the whole truth . . . In Chicago I was a person without a place; I belonged only to myself and learned to take care of only myself."

Yellowstone changed all that. Bostrom and her fellow YCC crewmembers worked hard and shared the burden. They tore down one of the wolf pens that wasn't needed anymore. The wolves were free now. Yellowstone was coming back to life, back to its ecological equilibrium. That summer, Bostrom and her cohorts discovered that national parks aren't just places—they're ideas. They're bravery, charity, and philanthropy. They're education, provocation,

contemplation, and inspiration, places where you learn to take care of not just yourself but also those around you, human and otherwise. You find out who you are and what you're capable of. You laugh, sing, hike, share, and think, all in the outdoors, the world's oldest health care clinic. When you hear scientists say that listening to two hours of nature sounds each day significantly reduces stress hormones by up to 800 percent and activates 500 to 600 DNA segments known to heal and repair the human body, you're not surprised.

Today, Bostrom is director of strategic partnerships and communications at Conservation Legacy, one of hundreds of nonprofits that partner with the National Park Service across America. Her colleague, Anthony "Chako" Ciocco of the Muscogee Indian Nation, takes tribal youths into parks and historic sites to build trails and restore streams. "It's hard, rewarding work," he says. "Some of these kids have face tattoos and knife wounds. They arrive guarded and sullen and end up making new friends, learning a lot. It works nearly every time. By helping to heal the Earth, they heal themselves."

Many participants in these programs end up finding careers in education and conservation. Some become professors or paramedics; others become park rangers. What might they aspire to? Consider 92-year-old park ranger Betty Reid Soskin at Rosie the Riveter/World War II Home Front National Historic Park in Richmond, California. "It's really a white woman's story," says Soskin,

**GRAND CANYON NATIONAL PARK | ARIZONA**

Sign up with Conservation Legacy and one thing is certain: you'll get your knees dirty. Founded in 1998, the Conservation Legacy continues the tradition of empowering students, veterans, and teachers to positively affect their lives, communities, and the environment.

who is African American and honored to share the Rosie story—how women by the thousands joined the workforce to help to win the war. In early 2009 Soskin attended the inauguration of President Barack Obama and carried with her a photograph of her great-grandmother, born a slave in 1846.

Consider Mary Beth Babtiste, who dusted off her wildlife biology degree, left her humdrum suburban life, and months later found her heart melting when she stroked the thick fur of a tranquilized grizzly bear in Grand Teton National Park. "For my life to matter," she wrote, "for me to do the work I'm meant to do in the world, I have to spend my days in mountains and forest like these, among people committed to their flourishing. And all they ask in return is a simple renunciation of everything I've ever known to be true."

............................................................................................................................

*"It is neither wealth nor splendor;*
*but tranquility and occupation*
*which give you happiness."*

## THOMAS JEFFERSON

............................................................................................................................

National parks don't require us to reinvent ourselves. They simply give us a window and a mirror in which to see ourselves—who we are, once were, and can be. They give us a canvas upon which to paint our imagination. They give us stories and deep time, history, and great sacrifice. They give us hope. They can be life changing, even life saving; always, they're life affirming.

One morning in 2004, a bus stopped near the new World War II memorial on the National Mall, dedicated to the "Greatest Generation"—16 million Americans who served in the U.S. military from 1941 to 1945. As a group of white-haired old men got out of the bus, many walking slowly, a few with canes, a passing jogger stopped and asked them if they were WWII veterans. Yes, they said. Not many WWII veterans remained. More than 1,000 were dying each day. Soon they'd all be gone. The jogger hugged them, one by one, and told them her grandfather had been liberated by American soldiers from a German concentration camp. They all ended up in tears. "Thank you," she told them. "You made the world a better place. Thank you for your service and sacrifice."

These days, dams aren't built in national parks; they're torn down. And with the dams gone, the salmon return. John Muir would like that.

Daniel Chure, a Park Service paleontologist at Dinosaur National Monument, loves to share his passion for fossils with visitors, especially children from the Make-A-Wish Foundation. He once asked an ailing boy, Nathan, to name his favorite dinosaur. Nathan told him it was *Compsognathus,* which was known from only two specimens. "He knew everything about it," Chure said, "how rare it was, how small it was, what it ate, where it lived. He could talk about it like a pro." When it came time to say goodbye, Chure handed Nathan his own prized cast of the dinosaur and said, "I've had this cast for several years and have enjoyed it, but you are the *Compsognathus* guy, and it should really be yours." The look in Nathan's eyes, Daniel said, was "unforgettable."

The unforgettable happens every day in America's national parks and other preserved sites. Every day brings revelations and affirmations, moments of great joy and simple truths. The land belongs to us, yes; but we also belong to it. "When taking down that wolf pen in the Yellowstone backcountry," concludes Bostrom, her voice confident, "we did not have a facilitator calling out the comparisons between an ecosystem and an urban community. Had there been, I would have tuned him out. I needed to learn from the land itself. I needed to seek connectedness and exploration much more than solitude and reflection . . . I needed to find a sense of belonging, and I did. We all did." ∎

**CUYAHOGA VALLEY
NATICNAL PARK | OHIO**

How to save our national parks? Make the parks relevant. Bring kids to the parks, and parks to the kids—into classrooms around the world. Teach the younger generation the magic and beauty of the natural world—the greatest show on Earth. This is the dream of every ranger.

**VALLES CALDERA NATIONAL PRESERVE | NEW MEXICO**

A massive authorization bill in 2014 began the transfer of this 89,000-acre preserve from the U.S. Forest Service to the NPS. "Our aim is to make the transition . . . as seamless as possible," said NPS Regional Director Sue Masica. This is the challenge: to move forward while also looking back.

# About This Book

*A Note on the Chronology*

HOW TO ORGANIZE A BOOK ON THE NATIONAL PARKS? Should it be by title: national parks, monuments, seashores, historical sites, battlefields, etc.? Or by region: East, West, North, South? Or geography: mountains, canyons, reefs, rivers, etc.? Or by year established? Any of these would work. Because this book is specifically the National Park Service's story—including the people who created our parks and the people who protect, share, and defend our parks today—the parks (also called "units") are organized by the order in which they became part of the National Park Service (NPS). This is not always when they were first recognized as a "park." Some were state parks or other designations before entering the NPS system. In addition, they specifically appear in the order of their first inclusion within the NPS, not upon redesignation, from "monument" to "park" for example.

Not every unit entered into the NPS system in the same manner. For example, Tennessee's Shiloh National Military Park was established in 1894 and transferred from the War Department to the NPS (part of the Department of Interior) in 1933. Arizona's Canyon de Chelly National Monument is administered cooperatively between the NPS and the Navajo Nation.

And not all NPS units share the same title—there are 22 types of National Park designations, such as national battlefield, national monument, national park, national seashore, etc. These designations are made by Congress when it passes legislation creating the park and generally do not affect their preservation.

Regardless of designation, the more than 400 parks and monuments and other sites exist for all to enjoy, as we hope you will this book. ■

# Acknowledgments

——◆◇◆——

NOT UNTIL I WORKED AS A RANGER for the National Park Service (NPS) did I believe I could do anything: climb mountains, run rivers, write books. Thank you to Tom Bredow, Virgil Olson, Bruce Paige, Bill Truesdale, Doug Cuillard, Hal Grovert, and Boyd Evison who took a risk and hired me (despite my long hair). Thanks also to Dr. Mike Folsom (professor of geomorphology), biologist/geologist Greg Streveler, historian William E. (Bill) Brown and anthropologist Richard K. Nelson, who inspired me. And to Don Chase, Jerry Case, Rick Caulfield, Dave Mills, Richard Steele, Larry and Karla Bright, Melanie (Neuman) Heacox, Jeffrey Hughes, Jim Shives (RIP), Bruce Talbot, Chuck Lennox, Rick McIntyre, Evan Jones-Toscano, Patty Brown, Denise Landau, and Leigh Selig (RIP), who shared the journey.

For this book (my fifth with National Geographic), I prospered from the expertise of NPS historians Robert (Bob) Sutton and John Sprinkle, and former NPS deputy director Denis Galvin, plus NPS director Jon Jarvis and his brother Destry, President, Outdoor Recreation and Park Services. My editor at National Geographic, Susan Straight, was patient, dedicated, and wise. Thank you also to Lisa Thomas for offering me this important book. As I finished the epilogue and reflected on a lifetime in national parks, my wife, Melanie, a ranger who mentors new NPS naturalists, said, "Everybody should find a landscape that they love beyond all reason, and devote themselves to it." I smiled.

KIM HEACOX,
Gustavus, Alaska
May 2015

**ALPHABET BLOCKS**
**LINCOLN HOME NATIONAL HISTORIC SITE, ILLINOIS**

These wooden blocks most likely served as the educational foundation for Abraham Lincoln's four children before tragedy struck and illness took three sons at early ages. Only Robert Todd Lincoln lived past his teenage years.

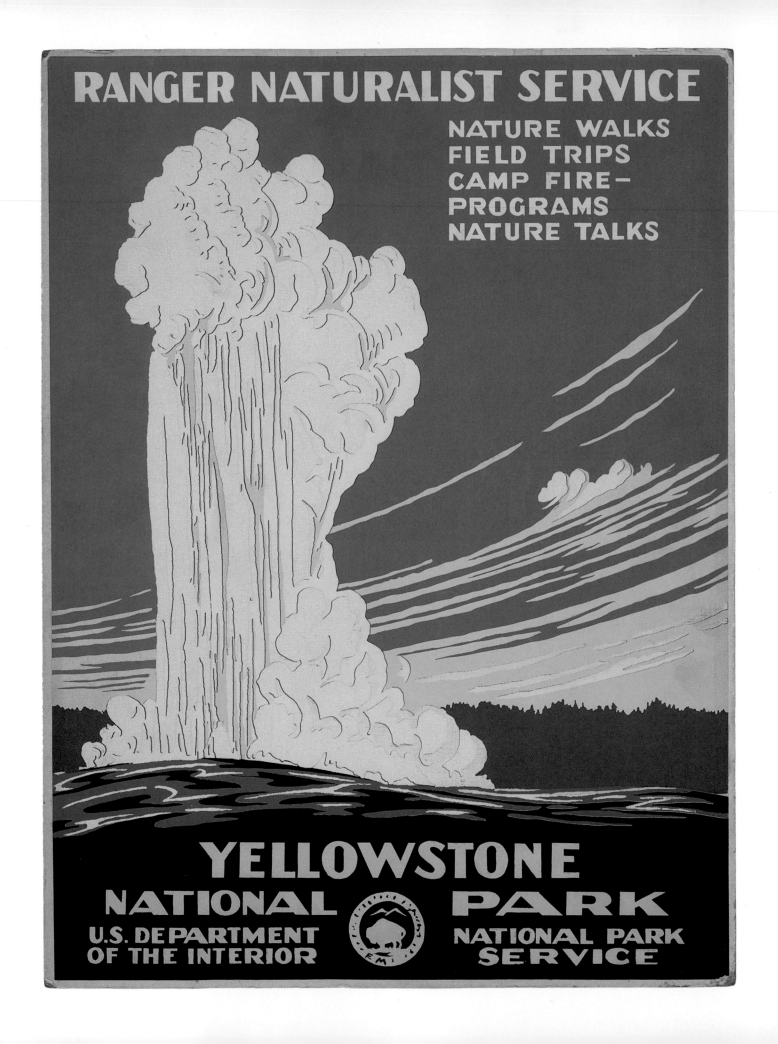

# National Park Properties

*In order of acquisition as of January 2015*

**1916** Yellowstone National Park

Sequoia National Park

Yosemite National Park

Mount Rainier National Park

Crater Lake National Park

Chickasaw National Recreation Area

Wind Cave National Park

Mesa Verde National Park

Devils Tower National Monument

El Morro National Monument

Montezuma Castle National Monument

Petrified Forest National Park

Chaco Culture National Historical Park

Muir Woods National Monument

Natural Bridges National Monument

Tumacacori National Historical Park

Navajo National Monument

Zion National Park

Salinas Pueblo Missions National Monument

Sitka National Historical Park

Glacier National Park

Rainbow Bridge National Monument

Pinnacles National Park

Colorado National Monument

Rocky Mountain National Park

Dinosaur National Monument

Acadia National Park

Hawai'i Volcanoes National Park

Capulin Volcano National Monument

Lassen Volcanic National Park

Abraham Lincoln Birthplace National Historical Park

**1917** Denali National Park

**1918** Casa Grande Ruins National Monument

Katmai National Park

**1919** Grand Canyon National Park

Scotts Bluff National Monument

Yucca House National Monument

**1921** Hot Springs National Park

**1923** Aztec Ruins National Monument

Hovenweep National Monument

Pipe Spring National Monument

Carlsbad Caverns National Park

**1924** Craters of the Moon National Monument

Bryce Canyon National Park

Wupatki National Monument

Hopewell Culture National Historical Park

**1925** Glacier Bay National Park

Lava Beds National Monument

**1926** Great Smoky Mountains National Park

Shenandoah National Park

Mammoth Cave National Park

**1929** Grand Teton National Park

Badlands National Park

Arches National Park

**1930** George Washington Birthplace National Monument

Colonial National Historical Park

**1931** Canyon de Chelly National Monument

Isle Royale National Park

**1932** Bandelier National Monument

Great Sand Dunes National Park

**1933** White Sands National Monument

Death Valley National Park

Black Canyon of the Gunnison National Park

Morristown National Historical Park

National Capital Parks

National Mall

White House

Ford's Theatre National Historic Site

**CLAY EFFIGY VESSEL
MESA VERDE NATIONAL
PARK, COLORADO**

..................................

The characteristic black-on-white pottery of the ancestral Puebloan played an integral role in trade and ceremonies. Today, color and materials variations allow archaeologists to more accurately date sites and document changes in cultural patterns.

*OPPOSITE:*
**PARK SERVICE POSTER
YELLOWSTONE NATIONAL
PARK, WYOMING**

..................................

Approximately one-half of the world's hydrothermal features are housed in Yellowstone, including more than 300 geysers, like Old Faithful.

## PLAYING CARDS
### GETTYSBURG NATIONAL MILITARY PARK, PENNSYLVANIA

..................................

Nervous and tired Union soldiers at Gettysburg were no doubt buoyed by the simple entertainment found in assistant surgeon Platte's patriotic pack of playing cards.

Rock Creek Park

George Washington Memorial Parkway

Washington Monument

Statue of Liberty

Lincoln Memorial

Cabrillo National Monument

Mount Rushmore National Memorial

Wright Brothers National Memorial

George Rogers Clark National Historical Park

Theodore Roosevelt Island

Chickamauga and Chattanooga National Military Park

Antietam National Battlefield

Shiloh National Military Park

Gettysburg National Military Park

Vicksburg National Military Park

Jean Lafitte National Historical Park and Preserve

Kennesaw Mountain National Battlefield Park

Guilford Courthouse National Military Park

Moores Creek National Battlefield

Petersburg National Battlefield

Fredericksburg and Spotsylvania County
    Battlefields Memorial National Military Park

Stones River National Battlefield

Fort Donelson National Battlefield

Brices Cross Roads National Battlefield Site

Tupelo National Battlefield

Cowpens National Battlefield

Appomattox Court House National Historical Park

Fort Necessity National Battlefield

Kings Mountain National Military Park

Big Hole National Battlefield

Castillo de San Marcos National Monument

Fort Matanzas National Monument

Fort Pulaski National Monument

Natchez Trace Parkway

Fort McHenry National Monument and
    Historic Shrine

Arlington House, The Robert E. Lee Memorial

Fort Washington Park

Gila Cliff Dwellings National Monument

Tonto National Monument

Jewel Cave National Monument

Olympic National Park

Oregon Caves National Monument

Devils Postpile National Monument

Walnut Canyon National Monument

Great Basin National Park

Timpanogos Cave National Monument

Chiricahua National Monument

Sunset Crater Volcano National Monument

Saguaro National Park

Cedar Breaks National Monument

**1934** Everglades National Park

Ocmulgee National Monument

Monocacy National Battlefield

Thomas Jefferson Memorial

**1935** Dry Tortugas National Park

Big Bend National Park

Fort Stanwix National Monument

Andrew Johnson National Historic Site

Jefferson National Expansion Memorial

**1936** Blue Ridge Parkway

Richmond National Battlefield Park

Homestead National Monument of America

Fort Frederica National Monument

Perry's Victory and International Peace
    Memorial

Whitman Mission National Historic Site

Joshua Tree National Park

Lake Mead National Recreation Area

Catoctin Mountain Park

Prince William Forest Park

**1937** Organ Pipe Cactus National Monument

Capitol Reef National Park

Cape Hatteras National Seashore

Pipestone National Monument

**1938** Salem Maritime National Historic Site

Channel Islands National Park

Saratoga National Historical Park

Fort Laramie National Historic Site

Hopewell Furnace National Historic Site

Chesapeake and Ohio Canal National
    Historical Park

NATIONAL PARK PROPERTIES

1939  Gulf Islands National Seashore

Federal Hall National Memorial

Independence National Historical Park

Tuzigoot National Monument

1940  Kings Canyon National Park

Manassas National Battlefield Park

Cumberland Gap National Historical Park

Little Bighorn Battlefield National Monument

Vanderbilt Mansion National Historic Site

1941  Fort Raleigh National Historic Site

1943  George Washington Carver National Monument

1944  Home of Franklin D. Roosevelt National
      Historic Site

Harpers Ferry National Historical Park

1946  Castle Clinton National Monument

Adams National Historical Park

Lake Roosevelt National Recreation Area

1947  Theodore Roosevelt National Park

1948  De Soto National Memorial

Fort Sumter National Monument

Fort Vancouver National Historic Site

Hampton National Historic Site

1949  San Juan National Historic Site

Saint Croix Island International Historic Site

Effigy Mounds National Monument

1950  Greenbelt Park

Fort Caroline National Memorial

1951  Grand Portage National Monument

1952  Christiansted National Historic Site

Coronado National Memorial

1954  Fort Union National Monument

1955  Pu'uhonua O Honaunau National Historical Park

Thomas Edison National Historical Park

1956  Booker T. Washington National Monument

Pea Ridge National Military Park

Horseshoe Bend National Military Park

Virgin Islands National Park

1958  Glen Canyon National Recreation Area

Lewis and Clark National Historical Park

General Grant National Memorial

1959  Minute Man National Historical Park

Franklin Delano Roosevelt Memorial

1960  Wilson's Creek National Battlefield

Bent's Old Fort National Historic Site

Arkansas Post National Memorial

Haleakala National Park

1961  Russell Cave National Monument

Cape Cod National Seashore

Fort Davis National Historic Site

Fort Smith National Historic Site

Piscataway Park

Buck Island Reef National
      Monument

1962  Lincoln Boyhood National
      Memorial

Hamilton Grange National
      Memorial

Whiskeytown Unit,
      Whiskeytown-Shasta-Trinity
      National Recreation Area

Sagamore Hill National Historic Site

Theodore Roosevelt Birthplace National
      Historic Site

Frederick Douglass National Historic Site

Point Reyes National Seashore

Padre Island National Seashore

1964  Ozark National Scenic Riverways

Fort Bowie National Historic Site

Allegheny Portage Railroad National Historic Site

Fort Larned National Historic Site

John Muir National Historic Site

Johnstown Flood National Memorial

Saint-Gaudens National Historic Site

Fire Island National Seashore

Canyonlands National Park

Bighorn Canyon National Recreation Area

1965  Curecanti National Recreation Area

Lake Meredith National Recreation Area

Nez Perce National Historical Park

Agate Fossil Beds National Monument

Pecos National Historical Park

Golden Spike National Historic Site

Herbert Hoover National Historic Site

Hubbell Trading Post National Historic Site

Alibates Flint Quarries National Monument

Delaware Water Gap National Recreation Area

Assateague Island National Seashore

Roger Williams National Memorial

Amistad National Recreation Area

1966  Cape Lookout National Seashore

Fort Union Trading Post National Historic Site

Chamizal National Memorial

San Juan Island National Historical Park

Guadalupe Mountains National Park

Pictured Rocks National Lakeshore

Wolf Trap National Park for the Performing Arts

Theodore Roosevelt Inaugural National Historic Site

Indiana Dunes National Lakeshore

1967  John Fitzgerald Kennedy National Historic Site

Eisenhower National Historic Site

**JOHN MUIR'S BINOCULARS
JOHN MUIR NATIONAL
HISTORIC SITE, CALIFORNIA**
..........................................

"Keep close to Nature's heart
. . . and break clear away,
once in a while . . . Wash your
spirit clean," Muir once told
friend and clergyman Samuel
Hall Young. He gifted these
binoculars to Young to better
appreciate nature's splendor.

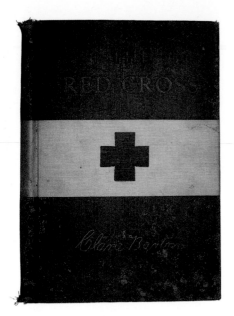

**THE RED CROSS IN PEACE AND WAR | CLARA BARTON NATIONAL HISTORIC SITE, MARYLAND**

.......................................

Clara Barton led by example when she stepped into the line of fire to bring Union soldiers much needed supplies and medical support. Her altruism spurred the creation of the American Red Cross in 1881, and her book (above) documents its humble beginnings.

| | |
|---|---|
| **1968** | Saugus Iron Works National Historic Site |
| | Appalachian National Scenic Trail |
| | Lake Chelan National Recreation Area |
| | North Cascades National Park |
| | Redwood National Park |
| | Ross Lake National Recreation Area |
| | Saint Croix National Scenic Riverway |
| | Carl Sandburg Home National Historic Site |
| | Biscayne National Park |
| **1969** | Florissant Fossil Beds National Monument |
| | Lyndon B. Johnson National Historical Park |
| | William Howard Taft National Historic Site |
| **1970** | Apostle Islands National Lakeshore |
| | Andersonville National Historic Site |
| | Fort Point National Historic Site |
| | Sleeping Bear Dunes National Lakeshore |
| **1971** | Voyageurs National Park |
| | Lincoln Home National Historic Site |
| **1972** | Buffalo National River |
| | Pu'ukohola Heiau National Historic Site |
| | Grant-Kohrs Ranch National Historic Site |
| | John D. Rockefeller, Jr. Memorial Parkway |
| | Longfellow House-Washington's Headquarters National Historic Site |
| | Hohokam Pima National Monument |
| | Thaddeus Kosciuszko National Memorial |
| | Cumberland Island National Seashore |
| | Fossil Butte National Monument |
| | Gateway National Recreation Area |
| | Golden Gate National Recreation Area |
| **1973** | Lyndon Baines Johnson Memorial Grove on the Potomac |
| **1974** | Big South Fork National River and Recreation Area |
| | Constitution Gardens |
| | Boston National Historical Park |
| | Big Cypress National Preserve |
| | Big Thicket National Preserve |
| | Clara Barton National Historic Site |
| | John Day Fossil Beds National Monument |
| | Knife River Indian Villages National Historic Site |
| | Martin Van Buren National Historic Site |
| | Springfield Armory National Historic Site |
| | Tuskegee Institute National Historic Site |
| | Cuyahoga Valley National Park |
| **1975** | Canaveral National Seashore |
| **1976** | Klondike Gold Rush National Historical Park |
| | Valley Forge National Historical Park |
| | Ninety Six National Historic Site |
| | Obed Wild and Scenic River |

| | |
|---|---|
| | Congaree National Park |
| | Eugene O'Neill National Historic Site |
| **1977** | Eleanor Roosevelt National Historic Site |
| **1978** | Lowell National Historical Park |
| | Chattahoochee River National Recreation Area |
| | War in the Pacific National Historical Park |
| | Fort Scott National Historic Site |
| | Ebey's Landing National Historical Reserve |
| | Edgar Allan Poe National Historic Site |
| | Friendship Hill National Historic Site |
| | Kaloko-Honokohau National Historical Park |
| | Maggie L. Walker National Historic Site |
| | Delaware National Scenic River |
| | Missouri National Recreational River |
| | New River Gorge National River |
| | Palo Alto Battlefield National Historical Park |
| | Rio Grande Wild and Scenic River |
| | Saint Paul's Church National Historic Site |
| | San Antonio Missions National Historical Park |
| | San Francisco Maritime National Historical Park |
| | Santa Monica Mountains National Recreation Area |
| | Thomas Stone National Historic Site |
| | Upper Delaware Scenic and Recreational River |
| | Aniakchak National Monument |
| | Bering Land Bridge National Preserve |
| | Cape Krusenstern National Monument |
| | Gates of the Arctic National Park |
| | Kenai Fjords National Park |
| | Kobuk Valley National Park |
| | Lake Clark National Park |
| | Noatak National Preserve |
| | Wrangell-St. Elias National Park |
| | Yukon-Charley Rivers National Preserve |
| **1979** | Frederick Law Olmsted National Historic Site |
| **1980** | Vietnam Veterans Memorial |
| | World War II Valor in the Pacific National Monument |
| | Boston African American National Historic Site |
| | Martin Luther King, Jr. National Historic Site |
| | Aniakchak National Preserve |
| | Denali National Preserve |
| | Gates of the Arctic National Preserve |
| | Glacier Bay National Preserve |
| | Katmai National Preserve |
| | Lake Clark National Preserve |
| | Wrangell-St. Elias National Preserve |
| | Alagnak Wild River |
| | Kalaupapa National Historical Park |
| | James A. Garfield National Historic Site |

Women's Rights National Historical Park

**1983** Natchez Trace National Scenic Trail

Potomac Heritage National Scenic Trail

Harry S Truman National Historic Site

**1986** Steamtown National Historic Site

Korean War Veterans Memorial

**1987** Pennsylvania Avenue National Historic Site

Jimmy Carter National Historic Site

El Malpais National Monument

**1988** Timucuan Ecological and Historic Preserve

Charles Pinckney National Historic Site

Natchez National Historical Park

National Park of American Samoa

Poverty Point National Monument

City of Rocks National Reserve

Hagerman Fossil Beds National Monument

Mississippi National River and Recreation Area

Bluestone National Scenic River

Gauley River National Recreation Area

**1989** Ulysses S. Grant National Historic Site

**1990** Petroglyph National Monument

Weir Farm National Historic Site

**1992** Niobrara National Scenic River

Mary McLeod Bethune Council House National
Historic Site

Salt River Bay National Historical Park and
Ecological Preserve

Manzanar National Historic Site

Marsh-Billings-Rockefeller National Historical Park

Dayton Aviation Heritage National Historical Park

Little River Canyon National Preserve

Brown v. Board of Education National Historic Site

Great Egg Harbor National Scenic and
Recreational River

Keweenaw National Historical Park

**1994** Mojave National Preserve

New Orleans Jazz National Historical Park

Cane River Creole National Historical Park and
Heritage Area

**1996** Boston Harbor Islands National Recreation Area

New Bedford Whaling National Historical Park

Nicodemus National Historic Site

Tallgrass Prairie National Preserve

Washita Battlefield National Historic Site

**1997** Oklahoma City National Memorial

**1998** Little Rock Central High School National
Historic Site

Tuskegee Airmen National Historic Site

**1999** Minuteman Missile National Historic Site

**2000** First Ladies National Historic Site

Rosie the Riveter/World War II Home Front
National Historical Park

Great Sand Dunes National Preserve

**2001** Virgin Islands Coral Reef National Monument

Minidoka National Historic Site

Governors Island National Monument

Craters of the Moon National Preserve

Flight 93 National Memorial

Cedar Creek & Belle Grove National Historical Park

World War II Memorial

**2005** Sand Creek Massacre National Historic Site

Carter G. Woodson Home National Historic Site

**2006** African Burial Ground National Monument

**2009** River Raisin National Battlefield Park

Paterson Great Falls National Historical Park

Port Chicago Naval Magazine National Memorial

**2010** President William Jefferson Clinton Birthplace
Home National Historic Site

**2011** Martin Luther King, Jr. Memorial

Fort Monroe National Monument

**2012** César E. Chávez National Monument

**2013** Charles Young Buffalo Soldiers
National Monument

Harriet Tubman Underground Railroad National
Historical Park

First State National Historical Park

**2014** Blackstone River Valley National Historical Park

Valles Caldera National Preserve

World War I Memorial

Tule Springs Fossil Beds National Monument

**2015** Pullman National Monument

Honouliuli National Monument

**TRUMAN'S WINGTIPS
HARRY S TRUMAN
NATIONAL HISTORIC SITE**

....................................

A haberdasher in the 1920s,
Truman was quite the dapper
president. He boasted 96
pairs of shoes in his collection
and matched them with finely
tailored suits made by friends
still in the business.

# Illustrations Credits

———◈◈◈———

LOC = Library of Congress, Prints & Photographs Division

NGC = National Geographic Creative

NPS = National Park Service

NPSMMP = National Park Service Museum Management Program

**Gatefolds:** (1-Sequoia), mosaic by Michael Nichols/NGC, compositing by Ken Geiger, NGS; (1-Yosemite), Mark Denton/Panoramic Images/NGC; (2-Canyonlands), Warren Marr/Panoramic Images/NGC; (2-Haleakala), Gary Crabbe. Front matter: 1, Harry Herzog, WPA Poster Collection, LOC, #3b48733; 2-3, Michael Melford/NGC; 4-5, Michael Nichols/NGC; 6-7, Yva Momatiuk & John Eastcott/Minden Pictures/NGC; 8-9, Phil Schermeister/NGC; 10-11, Michael Melford/NGC; 12-13, Rich Reid/NGC; 16, Marc Moritsch/NGC; 19, Courtesy NPSMMP and Frederick Douglass National Historic Site, FRDO 1895; 21, J. Baylor Roberts/NGC; 22, Courtesy NPSMMP and Lincoln Home National Historic Site, LIHO 2; 22-3, Courtesy RangerDoug.com; 23, Courtesy NPS; 24, Rich Reid/NGC; 25 (Musk Ox) FugeSpot/iStockphoto, (Bison) Rambleon/iStockphoto, (White-tailed Deer) mlorenzphotography/Getty Images, (Dall Sheep) twild-life/iStockphoto, (Burmese Python) Sergii Shalimov/Fotolia, (Moose) Wesley Aston/Shutterstock, (Blacktip Shark) Eric Isselee/Shutterstock, (Alligator) GlobalP/iStockphoto, (Nurse Shark) Mark Strickland/SeaPics.com, (Caribou) JackF/iStockphoto, (Black Bear) Joel Sartore/NGC, (Grizzly Bear) GlobalP/iStockphoto, (Wolf) Iakov Filimonov/Shutterstock, (Roosevelt Elk) Doug Lindstrand/Design Pics/Corbis, (Mountain Lion) GlobalP/iStockphoto, (Crocodile) Joel Sartore/NGC; 26 (A) Denali by Andy Gregg and Joel Anderson © 2015 Anderson Design Group, Inc. All rights reserved, (B) Death Valley by Michael Korfhage and Joel Anderson © 2015 Anderson Design Group, Inc. All rights reserved, (C & E) Contemporary poster design by Brian Maebius and Doug Leen © Doug Leen, (D & F) Lantern Press. **Chapter One:** 30-31, Carleton E. Watkins, LOC, #09988; 32, Educational Bruce Photograph/NGS Archives; 34 (UP-BOTH), U.S. Geological Survey; 34 (LO), Courtesy of the Yosemite Museum, Archives and Research Library, NPS; 35, Underwood & Underwood, LOC, #36413; 36, American Philosophical Society; 37 (BOTH), Portrait by Charles Willson Peale, Courtesy Independence National Historical Park; 38-9, Arthur C. Pillsbury/NGS Archives; 40, The White Cloud, Head Chief of the Iowas, 1844-45 (oil on canvas), Catlin, George (1796-1872)/National Gallery of Art, Washington DC, USA/Bridgeman Images; 41, Catalog #E73311, Department of Anthropology, Smithsonian Institution, Photo by Donald E. Hurlbert; 42, Carleton E. Watkins, LOC, #1s01345; 43 (UP), Bepsimage/iStockphoto; 43 (LO), Courtesy NPS; 44-5, Courtesy NPSMMP and Chaco Culture National

Historic Park (1) CHCU 33032, (2) CHCU 1262, (3) CHCU 31104, (4) CHCU 32334A, (5) CHCU 385, (6) CHCU 29079, (7) CHCU 1433, (8) CHCU 18550, (9) CHCU 92335, (10) CHCU 31204, (11) CHCU 30600; 46, LOC, #3b00011; 47 (UP), William Henry Jackson/U.S. National Archives; 47 (LO), Courtesy NPS, Yellowstone National Park, YELL 119144; 48-9, A. H. Barnes/NGS Archives; 50, Courtesy NPSMMP and John Muir National Historic Site, JOMU 3714; 51, Courtesy NPS, Yellowstone National Park, YELL 20; 52, F. H. Kiser/NGS Archives; 53, LOC, #36035; 54 (UP), John C. H. Grabill, LOC, #02642; 54 (LO), Courtesy NPS, Mesa Verde National Park; 55, Denver Tourist Bureau/NGS Archives; 56-7, Jim Richardson/NGC; 58-9, George Steinmetz; 60-1, Tom Murphy/NGC; 62 (LE), Stacy Gold/NGC; 62 (RT), Phil Schermeister/NGC; 63, Jim Brandenburg/Minden Pictures/NGC; 64-5, Phil Schermeister/NGC; 66-7, Melville B. Grosvenor/NGC; 68, Asahel Curtis/NGS Archives; 69, Design Pics, Inc/NGC; 70-71, David McLain; 72, Tom Till/Alamy; 73, Bates Littlehales/NGC; 74-5, Ira Block/NGC; 76, Yva Momatluk & John Eastcott/Minden Pictures/NGC; 76-7, Phil Schermeister/NGC; 78-9, Raul Touzon/NGC; 80, Clifton Adams/NGC; 81, Rich Reid/NGC; 82-3, Ira Block/NGC; 84-5, Keith Ladzinski/NGC; 86, Richard Nowitz/NGC; 87, Jonathan Kingston/NGC; 88-9, Marc Adamus; 90, Gavin Emmons/National Geographic Your Shot; 90-91, QT Luong/terragalleria.com; 92, Tim Fitzharris/Minden Pictures/NGC; 93, Lowell Georgia/NGC; 94-5, Tim Fitzharris/Minden Pictures/NGC; 96-7, Michael Melford/NGC; 98-9, Frans Lanting/NGC; 99, Chris Johns/NGC; 100, Courtesy NPS, Lassen Volcanic National Park; 101, Rich Reid/NGC; 102-103, Kelly Stone. **Chapter Two:** 104-105, Ansel Adams/Archive Photos/Getty Images; 106, Charles D'Emery/NGS Archives; 108, Great Northern Railway Historical Society; 109 (UP), Courtesy NPS, Casa Grande Ruins National Monument; 109 (LO), Scott J. Tanner collection; 110-111, Jasper D. Sayre/NGC; 112, U.S. National Archives; 113, Frank I. Jones/NGS Archives; 114 (UP), LOC, #3c36267; 114 (LO), Seattle Art Museum/Corbis; 115, Willis T. Lee/NGS Archives; 116, Courtesy NPS, Hopewell Culture National Historical Park, HOCU 2693; 117, Kolb Brothers/NGS Archives; 118-19, Courtesy NPSMMP and Vicksburg National Military Park (1) VICK 86, (2) VICK 1128, (3) VICK 1487, (4) VICK 1021, (5) VICK 1140_1561_1142, (6) VICK 168_1338_12_1372_159, (7) VICK 1146_1147_1148, (8) VICK 1831, (9) VICK 1040_1030_1034, (10) VICK 1903_1910; 120, Randall L. Jones/NGS Archives; 121, Courtesy NPS; 122 (UP), Courtesy NPSMMP and Guilford Courthouse National

**SCOTTY'S CASTLE ITALIAN PITCHER | DEATH VALLEY NATIONAL PARK, CALIFORNIA**

..................................

Duped into a poor gold mine investment by prospector Walter Scott, Chicago millionaire Albert Mussey transformed his desert land into an opulent vacation home. He and his wife furnished the house with the best handcrafted Mediterranean items money could buy.

Military Park, GUCO 349; 122 (LO), Melville B. Grosvenor/NGC; 123, Clifton R. Adams/NGC; 124-5, Annie Griffiths/NGC; 126-7, Ralph Lee Hopkins/NGC; 128-9, Roy Toft/NGC; 130-31, Ralph Lee Hopkins/NGC; 132, Phil Schermeister/NGC; 133, Pete Ryan/NGC; 134-5, Richard Nowitz/NGC; 136-7, Taylor Kennedy/NGC; 138-9, Sunny Awazuhara-Reed/Corbis; 140, Ralph Lee Hopkins/NGC; 141, Phil Schermeister/NGC; 142-3, Robert Sisson/NGC; 144, Greg Dale/NGC; 144-5, Greg Dale/NGC; 146-7, Robbie George/NGC; 148-9, Raul Touzon/NGC; 150, Roland W. Reed/NGS Archives; 151, Derek von Briesen; 152-3, Rich Reid/NGC; 154, Tim Fitzharris/Minden Pictures/NGC; 155, Tom Till/SuperStock/Corbis; 156-7, Commission of Fine Arts/NGS Archives; 158, James P. Blair/NGC; 159, Orren R. Louden/NGC; 160-61, Michael Melford/NGC; 162, Bruce Dale/NGC; 163, O. Louis Mazzatenta/NGC; 164-5, Kate Thompson/NGC; 165, Kate Thompson/NGC; 166-7, Tim Fitzharris/Minden Pictures/NGC; 168-9, Carr Clifton; 169, Phil Schermeister/NGC; 170-71, Dawn Kish/NGC; 172-3, Tim Fitzharris/Minden Pictures/NGC. **Chapter Three:** 174-5, Paul Zahl/NGC; 176, Walter A. Weber/NGC; 178, WPA Poster Collection, LOC, #3g01988; 179 (UP), W. H. Longley and Charles Martin/NGC; 179 (LO), Courtesy NPS, Everglades National Park; 180, NPS Historic Photograph Collection/photographer Roger W. Toll; 181, Walter A. Weber/NGC; 182-3, Willard Culver/NGC; 184, Courtesy NPSMMP and Cape Hatteras National Seashore, CAHA 107; 185, Bates Littlehales/NGC; 186 (UP), George F. Mobley/NGC; 186 (LO), Point Reyes National Seashore Museum, Catalog No. PORE 7876; 187, Walter Meayers Edwards/NGC; 188-9, Courtesy NPSMMP and Nez Perce National Historical Park (1) NEPE 1886, (2) NEPE 5720, (3) NEPE 2328, (4) NEPE 5339, (5) NEPE 2253, (6) NEPE 1254, (7) NEPE 1885, (8) NEPE 184, (9) NEPE 169, (10) NEPE 5337; 190, Walter Meayers Edwards/NGC; 191, NPS Historic Photograph Collection/photographer Jack E. Boucher; 192 (UP), Courtesy NPSMMP and Frederick Douglass National Historic Site, FRDO 25; 192 (LO), Bettmann/Corbis; 193, W. Robert Moore/NGC; 194-5, Carr Clifton; 196-7, Chris Johns/NGC; 198-9, Richard Nowitz/NGC; 200-201, Mike Theiss/NGC; 202, James L. Stanfield/NGC; 203, Larry Ditton/Danita Delimont/Alamy; 204-205, Tim Fitzharris/Minden Pictures/NGC; 206-207, Tim Laman/NGC; 208, NPS photo by Andrew Cattoir; 209, Gerry Ellis/Minden Pictures/NGC; 210-11, Steve Winter/NGC; 212-13, Norbert Wu/Minden Pictures/NGC; 213, Rich Reid/NGC; 214-15, Larry Carver; 216-17, Joel Sartore/NGC; 218, David Doubilet/NGC; 219, Todd Gipstein/NGC; 220-21, Michael Melford/NGC; 222-3, Tim Fitzharris/Minden Pictures/NGC; 224, Phil Schermeister/NGC; 225, Michael Melford/NGC; 226, Willard R. Culver/NGC; 227, 13/Christopher Robbins/Ocean/Corbis; 228-9, Pete McBride/NGC; 230-31, Tim Fitzharris/Minden Pictures/NGC. **Chapter Four:** 232-3, Dewitt Jones; 234, David Alan Harvey/NGC; 236 (UP), U.S. Department of the Interior, Bureau of Reclamation, Photo by J. D. Roderick; 236 (LO), Courtesy NPS, Yellowstone National Park; 237, NPSMMP and Lincoln Home National Historic Site, LIHO 367; 238, NPS Historic Photograph Collection/photographer Cecil W. Stoughton; 239 (UP), James P. Blair/NGC; 239 (LO), De Agostini Picture Library/Getty Images; 240-41, LOC, #349062; 242, Courtesy NPSMMP and Clara Barton National Historic Site, CLBA 933; 243, Henri Cartier-Bresson/Magnum Photos;

**GEORGE WASHINGTON INDEPENDENCE NATIONAL HISTORIC PARK | PENNSYLVANIA**

.....................................

Old and New Worlds clash in this folk art drawing, or fraktur, of George Washington. The medievalist style helped German immigrant artists preserve cultural ties while celebrating important subjects in their new lives in Pennsylvania.

# Index

# NATIONAL GEOGRAPHIC THE NATIONAL PARKS

## KIM HEACOX

**PREPARED BY THE BOOK DIVISION**

Hector Sierra, *Senior Vice President
and General Manager*
Lisa Thomas, *Senior Vice President
and Editorial Director*
Jonathan Halling, *Creative Director*
Marianne R. Koszorus, *Design Director*
R. Gary Colbert, *Production Director*
Jennifer A. Thornton, *Director of Managing Editorial*
Susan S. Blair, *Director of Photography*

**STAFF FOR THIS BOOK**

Susan Straight, *Editor*
Melissa Farris, *Art Director*
Meredith C. Wilcox, *Photo Editor*
Melanie Heacox, *Researcher*
Zachary Galasi, *Researcher*
Carl Mehler, *Director of Maps*
Matthew W. Chwastyk, *Cartographer*
Marshall Kiker, *Associate Managing Editor*
Judith Klein, *Senior Production Editor*
Mike Horenstein, *Production Manager*
Katie Olsen, *Design Production Specialist*
Nicole Miller, *Design Production Assistant*
Bobby Barr, *Manager, Production Services*

Since 1888, the National Geographic Society has funded more than 12,000 research, exploration, and preservation projects around the world. National Geographic Partners distributes a portion of the funds it receives from your purchase to National Geographic Society to support programs including the conservation of animals and their habitats.

National Geographic Partners
1145 17th Street NW
Washington, DC 20036-4688 USA

Become a member of National Geographic and activate your benefits today at natgeo.com/jointoday.

For information about special discounts for bulk purchases, please contact National Geographic Books Special Sales: specialsales@natgeo.com

For rights or permissions inquiries, please contact National Geographic Books Subsidiary Rights: bookrights@natgeo.com

Copyright © 2016 National Geographic Society.

Library of Congress Cataloging-in-Publication Data
Heacox, Kim.
National Geographic the national parks : an illustrated history / Kim Heacox.
pages cm
Includes index.
ISBN 978-1-4262-1559-9 (hardcover : alk. paper)
1. National parks and reserves--United States--History. I. National Geographic Society (U.S.) II. Title. III. Title: National parks.
E160.H39 2015
363.6'80973--dc23
2015014107

Printed in China

16/RRDS/3